the
SECRET LANGUAGE
of Puppies

the SECRET LANGUAGE of Puppies

THE BODY LANGUAGE OF YOUNG DOGS

Andrew Banks

METRO BOOKS
NEW YORK

METRO BOOKS
New York

An Imprint of Sterling Publishing
387 Park Avenue South
New York, NY 10016

Design by Ali Walper

ISBN 978-1-4351-5347-9

For information about custom editions, special sales, and premium and corporate
purchases, please contact Sterling Special Sales at 800-805-5489 or specialsales@
sterlingpublishing.com.

Manufactured in China

2 4 6 8 10 9 7 5 3 1

www.sterlingpublishing.com
www.quidpublishing.com

Conceived, designed and produced by
Quid Publishing
Level 4, Sheridan House
112-114 Western Road
Hove, BN3 1DD
United Kingdom

CONTENTS

INTRODUCTION

*O*wning and training a puppy is both a job and a joy, bringing with it rewards and responsibilities in about equal measure. Your day-to-day experiences with him, as well as the more formalized training you'll be practicing together in his first months, will determine the nature of your relationship. To get the most out of it you'll want to engage fully with him from the very first day.

TALK THE TALK

To get the best from your puppy, you need to understand what he's telling you. Dogs have been our domesticated companions for at least 10,000 years and maybe more, so it can sometimes seem surprising that we don't speak exactly the same language. Despite this, anyone with a loved and familiar pet will claim that they "know" what their dog is saying to them—and if dogs could speak, the chances are they would say that they too were quite confident about what humans' efforts to communicate were telling them. One of the many pleasures of getting a new puppy is the chance to become familiar with the messages that he sends you, and to watch him starting to understand what you are telling him, both with your voice and with your own body language.

BODY LANGUAGE: HIS AND YOURS

"Body language" is such a widely used phrase that we don't always think about what it means when we use it. As far as people are concerned, it covers anything that isn't conveyed by speech but is instead implied by the way we stand or gesture, or by our facial expressions. And although most people are fluent in human body language, few of us are aware of just how nuanced and subtle the body language of dogs can be—certainly as much as our own, if not more so. Dogs understand each other's body language intuitively, but if you want to learn it you need to study it, just as you'd have to learn any other language. And your new puppy can be your best teacher; he'll begin by using his own starter signals and build in eloquence until he can effectively send clear, fluent messages to any other dog. As he learns, you can extend your vocabulary in dog language, too.

Part of the Pack

Be skeptical when you're told that dogs are really wolves in domesticated clothing. While it's true that wolves and dogs have identical DNA, pet dogs have been bred through generations to perform a wide range of useful jobs, according to breed, and to live alongside humans as companions. The element that most experts agree remains instinctive in dogs is a preference for living socially, in a pack, which for today's pets is as likely to be a human pack as a dog one. It says a lot for the intrinsic adaptability of dogs that most pets will accept and accustom themselves to either option.

WATCH AND LEARN

Getting a puppy offers you the chance of a blank-slate relationship. Having a dog from eight weeks old is a huge opportunity to get to know another species from the start of his life. Telling him what you need him to do will always be an important aspect of the relationship; dogs live in the human world rather than the other way around, and as his owner and pack leader, it's your job to make sure that he learns to live comfortably in it. However, you may be surprised by all the ways you can learn from him and the extent to which your communication works in both directions, especially if this is the first dog you've had from a puppy. You're probably already familiar with the silent empathy a dog can offer during times of human stress and the exuberant way he will share and celebrate upbeat, happy moments; what may be new to you are the many different ways in which he can convey uncertainty, or invite play, or indicate that he's open to making a new acquaintance, whether canine or human. Take the time to observe him as well as interacting with him—you'll be surprised by how much you learn.

YOUR RESPONSIBILITY TO A PUPPY

Puppies are smart, but they're dependent on you to show them the ways of the world, and getting a puppy is a big responsibility. The first sections of this book will take you through what you can

expect to have to do both for and with your puppy, but what you get in return can far outweigh what you put in. Most dog owners would agree that no other species can offer as much in terms of one-to-one communication as a dog, and the complete familiarity you develop with a pet you've known all its life is hard to match with one that came to you as an adult.

If you have been careful and selective about where your puppy came from, he'll arrive as a healthy, cheerful, energetic youngster with an inquisitive attitude toward the world and an open, confident approach to training. And if you give him plenty of the same attitude back, staying upbeat and spending time getting to know his personality as well as making sure he's learning what he needs to know, he will learn faster when it comes to teaching him new things. His growing familiarity with your body language will help him to pick up what you want as you work together.

YOU'RE THE EXPERT

From the moment that you bring your new pet home, you'll find that you receive plenty of advice, most of it unsolicited. Suddenly, everyone's an expert. Unless the person giving it is a vet or someone you respect because you know they have a large amount of experience in raising and living with dogs, don't pay too much attention. Reading this book will give you a good grasp of the essentials, but the very best expert to learn from is your puppy himself. Within a couple of weeks you'll be familiar with the signs that tell you he's tired, hungry, or needs to go out. Another month or two and you'll have a clear idea of his favorite things to do and who and what makes him apprehensive or even frightened. And even if you don't have much previous experience with dogs and you're new to having a pet, watching him with other dogs will also teach you a lot about typical dog behavior in different situations, particularly in a group, and the ways in which your puppy is just being a dog, and those in which he's expressing his individual personality. As he comes to look to you more and more as his guide to the way the world works—the natural position for a human pack leader—you will understand more clearly when he can cope with a situation for himself and when you need to take the responsibility away from him and manage it because he's finding it a bit overwhelming. If you've spent plenty of

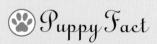

Puppy Fact

A puppy's first body language is learned around his mother and siblings. His first barks and tail wags are used to communicate with them; studies of puppies from very deprived or impoverished backgrounds with little interaction with either other dogs or people have shown that they use far fewer body-language signals than well-socialized puppies and may never become fluent users as adult dogs.

quality time with your puppy, both getting to know his personality traits and training and socializing him, by the time that he's an adult the communication between you will be so easy that you will hardly notice it anymore. This doesn't mean that any dog won't have personal idiosyncrasies or throw up the odd challenge—but as you know what to expect, so your relationship will relax, and it's then that you realize what people mean when they refer to their dogs as "one of the family." It's a feeling worth working for.

LEARN TO TEACH

Your puppy wasn't born knowing how to conduct himself politely in human society, and you weren't born with a natural knowledge of how to teach him to do so. Whether you're reading this just before you collect your new pet or he's already playing around your feet, you've got some hard work ahead. You can keep it straightforward by retaining your equilibrium and your sense of humor, and remembering at all times that if your puppy isn't learning right, it's probably because you're not teaching him well enough. If at some point you're trying to get him to master something and he doesn't seem to get it, despite repeated attempts, reread the steps, think them through, and then try again. Patience is (almost) everything when you're teaching, and if you sometimes have to take a minute of time out, that's fine.

A few decades ago, training a new puppy depended heavily on "dominating" him with the idea of forcing respect and breaking his will, and the recommended methods weren't always kind or even humane. Even today a lot of myths about dominance persist; steer clear of anyone who tells you to "make" your pet do anything. You want a cooperative partnership; you will never get it by force.

Modern training methods were developed partly because the idea of coercing a pet by force gradually became distasteful, and partly because of a growing respect for the dog as another species: wonderfully intelligent and adaptable, but with his own social rules and systems. Followed carefully, these methods will result in a pet dog who can both fit in with the human world in which he lives and still retain his full personality and functionality as a dog—the best outcome for everyone.

HAVE FUN

Finally, among all the necessary training and learning stages, never forget to have fun with your puppy. People and dogs aren't really all that similar, although they can achieve a good understanding, but one thing they have in common is an enthusiasm for play. You'll never have a more enthusiastic playmate than a young puppy; enjoy it, use it to build your relationship, play at least a little every day, and you really will have a friend for life.

No. 1 OWNING A PUPPY

RESPONSIBILITIES AND REALITIES

*I*t's pretty much universally agreed that puppies are cute. Less talked about is how much work caring for a puppy can be. They don't arrive as well-behaved companions—that takes time, and plenty of patience. Instead, they leave muddy paw prints on carpets, and chew shoes and pillows. It's up to you to help your pup grow into a well-mannered family member. There are also some things that are not changeable. A puppy will shed hair over your furniture and clothes, wake you up in the middle of the night to go out. and require care and attention 365 days of the year.

Consider fostering a dog from your local shelter for a few weeks. It can help you to decide if you have the resources to care for a puppy on a permanent basis.

Too many puppies end up in shelters. Many of these were adopted with the best of intentions, but their owners did not consider the responsibilities nor realities. It's a tragic situation for all involved, and one that you can avoid by evaluating the energy and commitment necessary.

IS THERE ANYONE HOME DURING THE DAY?

Puppies are sociable animals. Too much time alone makes for a frustrated, bored puppy, and that can result in behavioral issues. Puppies need people time—for walks, play, and training—every day.

Read any puppy forum online and you'll find owners who are struggling to meet the demands of their pup. Many find it stressful to arrive home after a busy day and be greeted by an overexcited pup and the mess he made while alone. Dinner needs to be made, or maybe there are kids who need help with homework. There are many things competing for your time, yet your puppy won't calm down. He's desperate for attention, and you feel overwhelmed and guilty for not being able to give it to him. This kind of situation makes for an unhappy puppy and owner.

What will you do to provide your pup with the companionship and mental and physical stimulation he needs daily? One solution may be hiring someone to come in to play with your pup and take him out for a walk. The amount of time your puppy is on his own each day will dictate how often this is necessary. A dog daycare is another possibility. It will contribute to the puppy's socialization (see chapter 9), while providing for his needs when you can't.

Your puppy will also need to be let outside during the day to relieve himself. How many times per day this will be necessary varies from pup to pup. However, it isn't unusual for a puppy to need to be taken out as frequently as once an hour while he's getting the hang of housetraining. And if there's no one to take him and he sometimes has to go indoors, it will also take longer to housetrain him reliably.

Puppy Fact

Your puppy will wake you early in the morning to be fed and to be let outside to relieve himself. Middle-of-the-night bathroom breaks are not uncommon.

the Border Collie and Dalmatian, will need more exercise than breeds with moderate exercise requirements, such as the Great Dane and French Bulldog.

Training: Teaching your puppy to respond to basic commands (see chapter 15) will build your bond. It's the only way your pup will learn acceptable behavior. The mental workout will also help keep him happy and calm.

DO YOU HAVE THE TIME AND ENERGY FOR A PUPPY?

Walks: It doesn't matter how tired you are or if you have the flu. It doesn't matter if it's raining or cold outside. Your puppy will still need to be walked.

Time in the yard or garden isn't a substitute for a walk. Walks do more than exercise your puppy physically; they expose your pup to other people and animals, cars, nature, and a variety of situations. Different sights, sounds, and smells stimulate your puppy's mind and help him feel comfortable in society.

Exercise: According to the UK Kennel Club, puppies need five minutes of exercise per month of age, up to twice a day. That would mean a six-month-old puppy needs approximately 30 minutes of exercise up to twice daily. It will vary according to a pup's breed and medical condition. High-energy breeds, such as

Puppies have short attention spans so training sessions should be brief. But to be successful count on at least 15–20 minutes, broken up into three sessions, each day.

Playtime: A pup will frequently play happily by himself but he also needs one-on-one interaction with you daily. It strengthens your relationship and provides mental and physical stimulation.

Play fetch using a soft chew toy—sticks can hurt a pup's mouth—or play hide and seek. Pups tire easily so keep sessions short, providing a break every 10 minutes or so.

Grooming: The amount of time needed will depend on your puppy's breed (see chapter 3). Double-coated breeds—such as the Border Collie, Golden Retriever, and Shetland Sheepdog—shed the most and will need daily brushing. Regular coat care is important for non- or low-shedding breeds as well. For example, many of the Terrier breeds shed little but their hair can easily become matted.

It's a good idea to establish a routine, even if your pup's coat doesn't need daily brushing. It helps your pup to be more comfortable with grooming sessions and provides

an opportunity for you to check his coat and body for any irregularities that could indicate a health concern.

HOW HOUSE-PROUD ARE YOU?

Your puppy will have housetraining accidents. He will chew your shoes and jump on furniture, at least until he is taught not to. He may also dig up your lawn and wee on plants.

All dogs shed in varying degrees; sharing your home with a puppy means accepting this. Even if you brush your puppy daily and vacuum regularly the reality is that there will be dog hair on your sofa and clothes.

DO YOU HAVE CHILDREN?

Do not buy a puppy to teach children responsibility. Although children can contribute to the brushing, feeding, and walking—once they have been taught how to safely interact with the puppy—ownership is a big responsibility that is best left to adults.

Small children should never be left unsupervised with a puppy. Children may have the best intentions but their energy level or enthusiasm can scare or hurt the pup, who may react by trying to protect himself or getting away.

The best pups for kids will be those that have a friendly and easygoing temperament. Size is also a consideration. In general, many toy-sized pups or small breeds need gentler handling than a child can provide. And pups that will grow to mid-sized or larger may do better around rambunctious kids. There are plenty of exceptions though, such as the Miniature Schnauzer or the Cavalier King Charles Spaniel—just two of the small breeds that can make good companions for children. Mutts can be a wonderful fit too. Again, look to their temperament when making a choice for your family. Is the pup friendly and curious? Or is he reserved and not very playful?

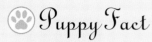

Some breeds are considered more family-friendly than others. But most pups can do well with children, as long as both are taught about appropriate behavior.

Shelter Pups

When a puppy ends up in a shelter it's not because he's a problem pup. Too often he is there because his owners failed him. They fell in love with his cuteness and gave him up when they realized the amount of training and care required. If you have the resources—time, energy, and finances—to care for a pup, consider adopting one from a shelter. You can make a real difference and gain a friend for life.

WHAT IS YOUR LIFESTYLE?

Think about this before you bring a puppy home. Are you looking for a pup you can curl up with or one who will—when he is a bit older—go hiking with you?

You should also consider how big the pup is expected to become. Will he be too large for your home or budget?

WHERE DO YOU LIVE?

Almost any dog can live happily in an apartment as long as they get the appropriate amount of exercise daily. Some are more suitable, however, particularly quiet and low-energy dogs. For example, your neighbors may not appreciate a Coonhound. Loving and gentle as this breed can be they're also high-energy and can be extremely loud —after all, they are a hunting dog that was bred to bark.

What is the climate like where you live? French Bulldogs and other flat-nosed, short-snout dog breeds—like the Pug or Shih Tzu—can have trouble breathing when the weather is hot and humid and may need air conditioning when the temperature rises. Double-coated breeds, like the Newfoundland, Akita, and Samoyed, are more prone to overheating and thrive in colder climates.

SHELTERS ARE OVERCROWDED

People give up on their puppies for various reasons:

- Their life changes—a new baby or job, for example—and they feel they don't have time for a puppy.
- They move, and relocating with the puppy is difficult.
- The pup sheds too much or makes the home untidy.
- They don't have the time for training and the pup misbehaves too often.
- The pup's activity level doesn't match their lifestyle. He's too laid back when they wanted a jogging partner, for example, or he's too high-energy when they wanted a lap dog.
- They didn't realize how much effort was involved in raising a pup.

Enter into puppy ownership only if you are sure you understand what it entails and can be there for the pup every day and also for the long haul.

DAILY SCHEDULE

This breakdown of what to expect from day to day serves as a guide, but remember that every pup is different.

GOING TO THE BATHROOM

As a general rule, the younger the puppy, the less control he will have over his functions. A conscientious breeder may have started housebreaking before you bring your puppy home, but expect a month or two at least of having to take him out around once an hour during the day. At night, when he's mainly sleeping, he will need to go less frequently, but you may still have to take him out once or twice.

WALKS

Puppies need less exercise than adult dogs but will still require a walk or two per day—for the exercise and socialization.

EXERCISE

How much exercise a puppy needs varies a lot, depending on his breed and energy levels. For example, a Border Collie is likely to tire much less easily than a Pekingese. Very small puppies don't need formal walks, but by the time your dog is six months old you should expect to be taking him out for walks a couple of times a day for around half an hour each time.

SLEEP

Growing puppies need a lot of sleep, much more than adult dogs. They may have bundles of energy at times but should rest as often as needed.

FOOD

Puppies should be fed small meals, three to four times daily. As they age this can change to twice daily.

BEHIND THE SIGNS

Key Terms

BREED: A classification that groups dogs based on their physical properties and temperament. Examples include the German Shepherd and Labrador Retriever.

SOCIALIZATION: The practice of introducing pups to different experiences so that they are more comfortable in everyday life.

TEMPERAMENT: A combination of mental, physical, and emotional traits.

CAN YOU AFFORD A PUPPY?

The adoption fees are just the start. Your pup will also need a leash, collar, and toys, and food will be a consistent expense for many years. Puppies need regular veterinarian check-ups and will occasionally need vaccinations. In case of an accident they may need a visit to an emergency or after-hours veterinarian clinic. There is a fee for puppy-training classes. You may need to pay for a boarding kennel, if you go on holiday or away on business. Some breeds, like Poodles, may require professional coatcare and clipping every month or two.

CAN YOU COMMIT TO A PUPPY FOR THE NEXT TEN OR MORE YEARS?

Your current situation may be ideal for bringing a puppy home. But what if your home, relationships, or work changes? If you suddenly need to move, are you willing to bring your puppy with you? It may mean that your housing options are limited to those that allow dogs. Or you may need to fly your puppy to wherever your new home is. If a new baby joins your family will you have the time and energy for a puppy? What if travel becomes part of your job? You are making a lifetime commitment when you bring a puppy home, regardless of the changes that may occur in your life.

WHERE TO GET YOUR PUPPY

SHELTERS, RESCUE ORGANIZATIONS, AND BREEDERS

*D*eciding where to get your puppy is a big decision, but with the right information it can be made a bit easier. There are plenty of choices, such as shelters and rescue organizations, breeders, or pet stores—although the latter should be avoided.

This chapter reviews your options, so you can get started on your journey toward sharing your home with a puppy.

SHELTERS AND RESCUE ORGANIZATIONS

Dogs of any age, from puppy to senior, and of any breed, from mixed to purebred, can be found at shelters and rescue organizations. Dogs are typically cared for by volunteers and are housed in onsite kennels or foster homes. Some rescue groups focus on a particular breed while others operate like most shelters, taking in any and all abandoned, abused, or stray dogs.

Myth: With shelter pups you never know what you are going to get.
Fact: Puppies don't know how to put on an act, so what you see is actually what you get. Of course, some training will be necessary, but that's true of any pup. Is the pup friendly or aggressive? A barker? High-energy or laid back? You'll know if you spend time visiting with the pup and speak with the shelter staff.

Prior to adoption, pups from reputable shelters and rescue organizations are:
• temperament- and behavior-tested
• vaccinated
• spayed or neutered

The organization should be able to answer questions about the pup's personality and the type of home he's best suited to. They will inform you about his health and activity level. They should also require an in-person screening interview to make sure you're a good match. All of this contributes to potential owners having a pretty good idea of what they are getting with a rescue pup.

Myth: Pups end up in shelters because something is wrong with them.
Fact: Most pups are in need of rehoming for reasons that have nothing to do with their behavior. According to the National Council on Pet Population Study and Policy in the US, the top four reasons dogs end up in shelters are:
1. The owners move away
2. There are landlord issues
3. The cost of pet maintenance
4. The owners have no time for their pet.

Shelter pups have been unlucky in terms of their owners, but they aren't unlovable.

Myth: A shelter pup comes with health problems.

Fact: There is no guarantee of health for any pup, regardless of where you get him. In well-run shelters puppies are vaccinated against disease, including DHPP (distemper/hepatitis/parvovirus/parainfluenza) and rabies. Pups are also treated for fleas or worms, if necessary (both are common to dogs anywhere).

Pups that are housed with lots of other dogs are susceptible to the kennel cough virus, but just like the coughs and colds people get kennel cough is easily treated.

Talk to the organization's staff and/or their veterinarian. If they are reputable (and that is easy to find out by searching for the organization online), you will be notified of any health concerns.

Myth: Shelter pups are unmanageable.

Fact: Each pup in the shelter is an individual. Some are very relaxed while others may be more excitable. It depends on their temperament, and the amount of training they have received.

Socialization (the practice of introducing pups to different experiences so that they are more comfortable in everyday life) also contributes to a pup's behavior. In a shelter pups play with other dogs and to get used to strangers. This can help them transition more easily when rehomed.

BEHIND THE SIGNS

Mixed Breeds

When you adopt a mixed-breed pup you get the benefit of two or more different breeds in one animal. Mixed breeds are less likely to have the health problems that can affect the body and behavior of a purebred pup. These problems result from inbreeding and can include orthopedic issues, such as hip dysplasia in the Saint Bernard, and behavioral issues, such as the constant digging of Terriers.

Myth: Rescue pups aren't purebred.
Fact: Many rescue organizations specialize in purebreds and these pups can also be found in shelters. Shelters may also have a mixed-breed pup with identifiable characteristics of the breed you are looking for.

Myth: You won't find a puppy at a shelter.
Fact: There are dogs of all ages waiting to be rehomed, including puppies. In fact, in some cases it's the "cuteness factor" puppies have that land them at the shelter. They may have been purchased or adopted because of their puppy charm, only to be abandoned when the reality of how much care a puppy needs set in.

To find a shelter near you search online for "humane society," "animal control agency," or "animal shelter." It may also be known as a rescue or rehoming center, depending on where you live.

BEHIND THE SIGNS

Is Your Heart Set on a Purebred Pup?

Many people are surprised to find that purebred puppies can be adopted through rescue organizations and shelters. In fact, the ASPCA (American Society for the Prevention of Cruelty to Animals) reports that one in four shelter dogs are purebred.

Breed characteristics can help you anticipate a puppy's temperament but they don't define him. He's still his own dog.

Do you spend your weekends hiking? A Bernese Mountain Dog may be your perfect match. Will you have time for the daily brushing their long, silky coat requires? A Doberman Pinscher is another option. They also enjoy hiking and their short coat needs only minimal grooming.

There's a reason the Golden Retriever is known as a good family dog. They're loyal, easy to train, and good with children. But don't make a decision about the breed of your puppy until you learn about other breeds as well. For instance, the Cardigan Welsh Corgi is an affectionate and even-tempered dog who enjoys time with his family.

Are you looking for a dog that you can cuddle up with? It's a favorite pastime of the Chihuahua. They're also great apartment dogs. If you're not interested in one of the toy breeds, what about a bloodhound? This large breed of dog likes lots of affection. The bloodhound can be loud though, so he's better suited to a home where the neighbors are not close enough to hear his impressive "bay"—a melodious or irritating cry, depending on the listener.

🐾 Puppy Fact

A puppy is shaped by his breed characteristics and the people in his life.

HOW MANY BREEDS OF DOG EXIST?

It's difficult to give an exact number because kennel clubs and breed registration groups differ in the breeds they recognize. All put certain breeds together into a "breed group," but this is done according to the organization and is not the same worldwide.

The American Kennel Club recognizes 178 breeds of pedigree dog, classified as Sporting, Hound, Working, Terrier, Toy, Non-sporting, or Herding.

The Kennel Club (UK) recognizes 210 breeds of pedigree dog, classified as Hound, Working, Gundog, Terrier, Utility, Pastoral, or Toy.

They, like national organizations in other countries, may choose to add to the list of breeds they recognize, if a breed has the necessary history and documentation, and there is enough interest in the breed.

The Fédération Cynologique Internationale (FCI, less frequently known as The World Canine Organization) is an international federation of kennel clubs. They recognize 339 breeds and use ten breed groups to classify them:

1. Sheepdogs and Cattle Dogs (except Swiss Cattle Dogs)
2. Pinscher and Schnauzer—Molossoid Breeds—Swiss Mountain and Cattle Dogs
3. Terriers
4. Dachshunds
5. Spitz and Primitive types
6. Scenthounds and Related Breeds
7. Pointers and Setters
8. Retrievers—Flushing Dogs—Water Dogs
9. Companion and Toy Dogs
10. Sighthounds

BEHIND THE SIGNS

Report Card

Full pedigree dogs at professional shows and breed competitions are judged by a breed standard. This includes minute specifications for a breed "ideal," covering everything from permitted variations in coat color to height, build, ear position, and overall "conformation," or body build and structure. If you think you might be interested in showing your puppy professionally later on, be sure to discuss your ambitions with the breeder—a show dog must not only conform to the standard for its particular breed, but also needs a steady, easygoing temperament.

BREED GROUPS IN BRIEF
Gundog and Sporting Groups

Bred for hunting and other sporting activities, these athletic dogs have high exercise needs—typically an hour per day. They are faithful and even-tempered dogs who thrive in the company of their family. Grooming requirements vary by breed. Examples include the:

- American Cocker Spaniel
- Brittany
- English Setter
- German Shorthaired Pointer
- Gordon Setter
- Hungarian Vizsla
- Labrador Retriever
- Nova Scotia Duck-Tolling Retriever
- Weimaraner
- Welsh Springer Spaniel

Herding and Pastoral Groups

These dogs were bred to work sheep, cattle, and other livestock. They need plenty of daily exercise—up to an hour per day or more, depending on breed—and are easily bored if they don't get enough mental and physical stimulation. Protective and intelligent, these dogs are not the type to sit back and watch; they want to join in activities with their family. They require regular brushing, either daily or a few times a week. Examples include the:

- Belgian Tervuren
- Border Collie
- Briard
- Finnish Lapphund
- German Shepherd Dog
- Icelandic Sheepdog
- Pembroke Corgi
- Puli
- Pyrenean Mountain Dog
- Samoyed
- Shetland Sheepdog

Hound Group

Originally bred for hunting, the dogs in this group are known for their remarkable ability to follow a scent and their impressive endurance while tracking. Other than that, it's a diverse group. Some of these dogs can be stubborn at times, which makes sense as they were bred to work independently to find their quarry. Many are friendly and affectionate, while others are more aloof. Most are equally happy on long walks or curled up by the fire. Examples include the:

- Afghan Hound
- Basset Hound
- Beagle
- Bloodhound
- Dachshund
- Finnish Spitz
- Greyhound
- Irish Wolfhound
- Rhodesian Ridgeback
- Whippet

THEY DO *WHAT?*

Dogs are astonishingly varied and adaptable. Just look through the following breed facts:

- The Lagotto Romagnolo breed is a truffle-hunter.
- Although known as the "barkless dog," the Basenji does use his voice if he's excited—he makes a noise like a yodel.
- Dalmatian puppies are born with a white coat. Their spots start to appear at about three weeks old.
- The Nova Scotia Duck Tolling Retriever lures waterfowl close to the shore by using his waving, white-tipped tail.
- The Alaskan Malamute has been a sled dog longer than any other dog of the working group.
- The Newfoundland breed has a water-resistant coat and webbed feet, handy since they were bred for water rescue and to haul fishing nets.
- Bloodhounds are natural born detectives and have been known to get results even when the tracks followed were over 300 hours old.
- Greyhounds are the second fastest land animal on earth.

A Range of Uses

The Utility or "Non-Sporting" group is the joker in the dog groupings pack. Unlike the members of the other groups, who generally share many characteristics and often were bred for similar jobs, its members are very varied indeed—and were originally used to do a wide range of work, too. The elegant Dalmatian, for example, was originally called "the carriage dog" as it was bred to run alongside gentlemen's carriages, while the Chow Chow is one of the oldest breeds still in existence and was used to guard temples in Ancient China.

Non-Sporting or Utility Groups

This group includes dogs of different sizes, temperaments, and activity levels. It includes some of the oldest breeds. Examples include:

- Akita
- Bichon Frise
- Bulldog
- Chinese Shar-Pei
- Chow Chow
- Dalmatian
- Lhasa Apso
- Poodle
- Shih Tzu
- Tibetan Terrier

MIXED BREEDS

This chapter may be devoted to purebred dogs but it's important to mention mixed breeds too. They have so much to offer. In fact, many people would not consider any other type of dog because:

- If a dog's needs are met in a caring environment he will return the favor with love and loyalty, and he doesn't need a pedigree to do so.
- Any dog, regardless of ancestry, can become a cherished part of your family. You provide the tools for this: socialization, training, and lots of affection.
- A mixed-breed dog has parents from two different purebred, or from mixed-breed, dogs and shares characteristics from both. That can make a great combination.
- Shelters and rescue organizations have many wonderful mutts in need of a good home.

BEHIND THE SIGNS

New Breeds

In the mid-1950s, a poodle was crossed with a labrador to create the Labradoodle. The specific intention in that case was to breed a service dog with a poodle-type coat that wouldn't trigger allergies, but since then some specific breed mixes—with names to match—have become increasingly popular. You've probably heard of the Spoodle and the Cockerpoo, but there are literally dozens of others. Puppies of the most popular, particularly the Labradoodle, cost as much as many single-breed pups, and some clubs for these crosses are pushing the official kennel clubs to include them in their official breed lists in their own right.

Terrier Group

The earliest Terriers were bred to rid farms of vermin, such as mice and rats, and to dig down and drive larger animals such as foxes from their burrows (hence the name, from *terra*, the Latin word for "earth"). They are mostly small- to medium-sized and are known for their feisty and independent attitude. Cheerful and energetic, they tend to need a lot of exercise for their size and most will need mental stimulation too. They're best suited to an active lifestyle. Examples include the:

• Airedale Terrier
• Australian Terrier
• Border Terrier
• Cairn Terrier
• Fox Terrier
• Kerry Blue Terrier
• Lakeland Terrier
• Miniature Schnauzer
• Staffordshire Bull Terrier
• Welsh Terrier

Toy Group

They may be small but they're no pushovers. These dogs have lots of dignity, and can be tough when they feel it's necessary. Mischievous and affectionate, they make ideal pets as they don't need a lot of room and you can take them anywhere. Their short legs make even a walk around the block a good workout, and indoor play takes care of the rest. Examples include the:

- Brussels Griffon
- Cavalier King Charles Spaniel
- Chihuahua
- Maltese
- Papillon
- Pekingese
- Pomeranian
- Pug
- Shih Tzu
- Yorkshire Terrier

 *Puppy Fact*

The skills for which your pup was bred may no longer be necessary, but he'll still have an instinctive need to "work." You can see this in the way a dog of the herding group will affectionately herd his people family, or a dog from the hound group will track a scent to its source.

 Puppy Fact

There are small breeds in every group, not just the toy group.

Toy-Breed Puppies

Generally bred exclusively for companionship, most toy breeds are very small, and it follows that their puppies may be very tiny indeed. If you choose a Chihuahua or a Pomeranian, your pup will be more fragile than many of the larger breeds, and you'll need to be especially careful when he's underfoot or being handled by children.

Working Group

These dogs were originally bred to perform search and rescue, and as messenger, guard, or sled dogs. As you'd imagine, they're protective and possess strength and endurance. They're also intelligent and loveable family pets. Their exercise needs are breed-specific. Examples include:

- Alaskan Malamute
- Bernese Mountain Dog
- Boxer
- Canadian Eskimo Dog
- Great Dane
- Great Pyrenees
- Newfoundland
- Portuguese Water Dog
- Siberian Husky
- St. Bernard

FIND YOUR PERFECT COMPANION

Before you bring home that adorable puppy, sit down and write out all of the characteristics that are most important to you in a dog. They might include: adventurous, easygoing, enthusiastic, faithful, independent, intelligent, loving, protective, and sociable.

Think about the size of dog that best suits you. Consider how much time you can devote to exercise needs and grooming requirements. Don't just consider the puppy, but also the dog he will grow into. With so many breeds available, each with their own characteristics, you'll find your match.

To help narrow down your search, the following examples illustrate what you should consider, and the variety of breeds available.

Coat care

The Komondor breed has a stunning white cord coat. Keeping it that color can be a challenge though, as it easily shows dirt. A bath or swim might wash the dirt away, but the cords can take over 12 hours to dry. The coat will also need brushing a few times a week. Taken all together, that's a high-maintenance coat. In contrast, the elegant Whippet has minimal grooming needs. His short coat only needs to be brushed once a week.

Ask yourself how much coat care you're able to give your dog.

Energy level

All dogs will need regular exercise. A high-energy breed may need at least an hour per day. Without the energy outlet and stimulation that exercise provides these dogs can become destructive or exhibit other behavioral problems. Toy breeds need less exercise, as is true of larger breeds. Ask yourself how much exercise you can commit to each day.

Shedding

Dogs shed, and those with dense double coats, such as the Samoyed, Newfoundland or Alaskan Husky breeds, shed a lot. The Airedale Terrier or the Irish Water Dog, among others, shed minimally. Ask yourself how much shedding and cleaning up of hair you can live with.

Size

Think about the adult size the puppy you're considering will grow to. If your home is small the Great Pyrenees is not a good match, not because of how big he is but because of how much space he likes to have to move around in. The Greyhound, tall as he is, can be happy in a small apartment, as long as his daily exercise needs are met. Do you want a small, medium, or large breed?

Sociability

Some breeds are affectionate with their human family, but aloof with strangers. Others are best suited to a certain type of home. The Chihuahua, for example, may not get along with small children. Many other breeds can step in for him, including the Bull Terrier, Newfoundland, Collie, and the Bulldog—all known to form strong bonds with kids. The Bulldog usually coexists well with cats but may not get along with another dog in the house. A Chow Chow (often described as having a cat-like personality) may not get along with another canine.

If you're considering a puppy and are worried about sociability, observe the pup with others and interact with him. As long as he has been socialized, and continues to be when you go home, it shouldn't be an issue.

A GUIDE TO BUYING OR ADOPTING

*Y*ou've decided where you want to get your puppy (see chapter 2) and now it's time to visit the shelter or breeder and start the selection process. Know that it can take many visits before you decide on a puppy. Although it's not easy to leave empty-handed—in fact, studies have shown that the puppy cuteness factor plays upon our instincts to provide care—it's too large a decision to rush. The puppy you take home is a long-term commitment of a decade or longer.

SHELTER: BEFORE YOUR VISIT

Before you visit a shelter, you should find out the following:

- Ask what time the pups are most awake and schedule your visit then.
- Find out what their policies are regarding: observing the pups interacting with each other; and spending one-on-one time with the pup you are interested in, away from the others (many shelters have a visiting room for this purpose).
- Prepare your list of questions:
  1. Do you have information on the pup's history?
     Was he a stray? Did his owners surrender him to the shelter? Most shelters require that owners who give up their dogs provide information on the dog's health and behavior.
  2. How long has the pup been at the shelter?
  3. How does the pup interact with others (including other dogs or children)?
  4. Does the pup have any behavioral issues?
  5. Is the pup housebroken?
  6. What are the pup's daily coat-care and exercise needs?
  7. Has the pup been neutered or spayed?
  8. What type of temperament test was performed on the pup and what were his results?

SHELTER: ON YOUR VISIT

Once you've arrived at the shelter, it's important to keep in mind the criteria you've decided upon and to make sure you ask all the questions you have prepared. Talk to the shelter staff or breeder about which pup or pups may be a good match for you.

Plan to spend at least 30 minutes or more observing and interacting with each puppy you are considering, so you can see how they socialize with others and with you. Perform your own temperament test (a sample is provided in this chapter).

FIND A BREEDER

Reputable breeders don't advertise in newpapers or online and they don't sell to pet shops. They may not have a pup available as soon as you make an inquiry, because they breed only when they have a waiting list of interested puppy buyers.

Your veterinarian or local breed clubs should be able to recommend breeders, and they can also be found by attending professional dog shows for the breed you're interested in.

QUESTIONS TO ASK THE BREEDER
What are this breed's health issues?

Genetic problems exist for almost every breed. The breeder you want is one who will be honest about this and explain the steps taken to reduce passing on problems to the litter. For example, many large breeds suffer from joint and bone disorders such as hip dysplasia, while many short-faced (known as brachycephalic) breeds suffer from breathing problems. Good breeders screen potential parents before breeding.

What guarantee do you provide?

The breeder should state in writing what their responsibilities are in case of a congenital ailment. Typically this would involve giving you your money back or taking the puppy back and giving you a different one. They should also state that they will take the puppy back if for some reason you can't keep him. This type of guarantee is an indication of a responsible breeder.

What dog clubs or organizations do you belong to?

Many national clubs, such as the American Kennel Club and the Kennel Club (UK), and local organizations have a code of ethics that breeders are required to follow.

How long have you been involved with this breed?

It may be a warning sign if the breeder has switched breeds frequently (for example, following popularity trends for breeds) or if they have multiple breeds. You want someone who is invested in and dedicated to the breed you are looking for.

How often do you breed?

If the mother (dam) is being bred every heat cycle it's too often. A breeder who has the best interest of dogs in mind would not do that.

How well do the parents conform to the breed standard?

The breeder should be an expert on the breed and able to discuss this with you in detail. Even if you're not looking for a show-quality puppy the breeder should use the best examples of the breed in their breeding programme. Ask to see the pup's pedigree. It should have show and working titles within the first two generations.

What is the pup's medical history?
This should include the vaccinations appropriate to the age of the puppy (see chapter 12) and deworming. All pups are born with worms, so the latter treatment shouldn't alarm you—it's normal.

How have the pups been socialized?
Good breeders will introduce pups to different people, environments, and sounds—from children to the sound of a washing machine—so that they are well adjusted and comfortable in everyday life. Socialization must start by six weeks of age and continue from there.

Have the pups been temperament tested?
Each pup should be evaluated as to temperament: aggressive, easygoing, high-energy, responsive, shy, or strong-willed (and quite often a pup will exhibit traits of more than one temperament type).

The breeder should be happy to answer any questions; it shows you have done your homework and are serious about caring for a pup. The breeder will also have plenty of questions for you. You should be asked about your home, family, and daily life so that the breeder can place the pup where he will get all of the care and love he needs to thrive.

BEHIND THE SIGNS

Talking to the Breeder

Take someone knowledgeable with you on your visit to the breeder, or do your research on breed standards before you visit. The website for the national kennel club organization where you live is a good place to start. Most list breed standard information.

TEMPERAMENT TEST

Shelters and breeders use a variety of temperament tests to learn more about a puppy's personality, particularly qualities such as dominance, independence, and fearfulness. It is important to remember that a pup's temperament is made up of many different traits, not just one. The following exercises can help you get to know the puppy you're interested in:

1. Hold the pup in your arms like you would a baby and look directly into his eyes.
2. Hold the pup under his armpits so that he is facing you (his legs should be dangling) and look him in the eye.
3. Stand behind the pup and lift him slightly off the floor by holding him around his midsection.

Results: If the pup is comfortable, it's usually a sign that he's easygoing and will be happy taking direction from you. If he resists it's an indication he's strong-willed; these types of pups typically need an experienced dog owner and one who will treat him with a loving but firm hand.

4. Slowly back away from the pup, then hold out a treat and call him.

Results: If he runs to you happily it's a sign that he's self-assured and friendly. If he needs coaxing he may be shy or fearful.

5. When the pup is busy playing with a toy or looking elsewhere, jangle a large set of keys over his head.

Results: If he jumps up playfully or just glances at the keys and continues playing it's a sign he's composed and even-tempered. If he cowers he may be highly strung or fearful.

6. Leave the room and watch how the pup reacts to being left alone.

Results: If the pup whines and cries he may be shy or fearful. Confident, assertive pups may not pay much attention.

7. From a standing position, lean over to pet the pup.
8. Sit down, place the pup between your knees and pet him.

Results: If the pup relaxes and lets it happen he is happy to interact. If he nips at you or tries to move away he may be more aloof or frightened.

THE BREEDER'S FACILITY

You should be welcome to visit. If a meeting place, other than where the pup was born, is suggested instead it may be a warning sign that there's something they don't want you to see (for example, a puppy mill).

Evaluate the environment:

Does it appear clean and well run?

Observe the other dogs on site:

Do they look well cared for and happy?

Meet the dam of the litter:

She may be a little nervous about having strangers near her pups, but overall she should appear well adjusted and healthy.

WHEN YOU HAVE SELECTED A PUPPY

Congratulations! Asking the shelter or breeder the following questions can help your pup settle into his new home:

- What type of food has the pup been eating? How much is he fed daily and when?
- What type of potty schedule has the pup been on?
- Has the pup had any training and, if so, what command words does he respond to?
- Is the pup comfortable being groomed?
- Does the pup have a favorite toy or blanket?

QUESTIONS YOU MAY BE ASKED

To make sure that they are placing the pup in the right home, the shelter or breeder may ask questions about your life, such as:

• Do you live in a house or an apartment?

• Do you own your home and, if not, does your lease agreement allow pets?

• How long have you lived in your home?

• Do you have children?

• Do you have experience with dog ownership?

• Do you have pets?

• Who will be the primary caretaker of the puppy?

• How many hours each day will the pup be left on his own?

• How much time can you provide for the pup's exercise and grooming needs?

• Where will the pup sleep?

Puppy Fact

No reputable breeder would separate a pup from his mother before eight weeks of age.

Key Terms

TEMPERAMENT: A combination of mental, physical, and emotional traits.

TEMPERAMENT TEST: Handling exercises that are used to provide insight into a pup's personality (for example, to determine if he is assertive or passive).

MEETING A PUPPY

When you meet a litter of puppies you'll notice that each one has his or her distinct personality, even at just a few weeks old. Some are livelier than others and some are evidently fearful of new experiences; others may be confident or even feisty. You're likely to have limited time with a litter, and it's tricky to generalize about what individual body language means on the basis of a single short session, but here are some of the signs you may notice—and what they may tell you about a puppy. You'll find a more detailed guide to puppy body language in chapter 13.

REACTIVE

A sensitive but strong reaction to a new situation—a puppy may put on a display of teeth or the hackles (hair) on the back of his neck may stand up if he feels he is being challenged.

WHAT YOU SEE
This pup's tail, ears, and the hair on the back of his neck and along his shoulders may rise—all to make him look bigger and taller. His eyes may narrow, and his lips pull back to show his teeth. He may lean forward ready to lunge if he feels it's necessary.

WHAT TO DO
Stay still, don't make direct eye contact, and don't reach out toward the puppy. He's showing signs that he feels threatened by you, and he's preparing to defend himself. You don't want to push him into action.

WHAT IT MIGHT INDICATE
A strongly reactive puppy who feels threatened by new situations and decides to take matters on himself isn't a good choice for a first-time owner, particularly if you're proposing to house him with other dogs or with children. He'll need structured training to accustom him to the idea that he should take guidance from his owner and rely on them to take care of situations that worry him.

SHY

When a puppy seems very placid or even a little timid, he may be naturally happy to take his guidance from those around him, or it may be a cover for a slightly fearful reaction to unfamiliar experiences.

WHAT YOU SEE
He may tuck his tail in, look away from you, or roll on his back on meeting you. He's showing the appeasement signs he would offer an adult dog to remind it that he's small and young, and not a threat.

WHAT TO DO
Let the puppy approach you in his own time—don't crowd him. When he does approach, keep your hands where he can see them and pet him very gently.

WHAT IT MIGHT INDICATE
A puppy who's happy to take guidance is often easy to train with plenty of positive reinforcement to build his confidence, and will naturally look to his owner for a lead on how to behave.

CONFIDENT

A puppy who's enthusiastic about engaging with strangers and who responds to new noises or touches with happy curiousity is sending positive all-round signs.

and eager to embrace what life has to offer him. He already interacts well with people, which is likely to make him easy to train.

WHAT YOU SEE
A puppy who approaches you happily, tail up, and immediately engages with you, responding to petting or cuddling with gusto.

WHAT TO DO
Enjoy interaction with the puppy as much as he's enjoying interaction with you.

WHAT IT MIGHT INDICATE
These are good signs that the puppy is well balanced

ASSERTIVE

A puppy who has a strong character may be used to coming top of the heap in the litter, getting first pick on valued resources, such as food and toys.

WHAT TO DO
Attract the puppy with a whistle or other noise, then watch the way he approaches and behaves with you. See if he easily gives a toy up to you.

WHAT YOU SEE
In the rough-and-tumble of puppy interaction, this is the pup who gets to most things first, and will confidently take what he wants from his siblings.

WHAT IT MIGHT INDICATE
This may be a strong-minded pup who needs plenty of training, but it's a positive sign that he doesn't show any fear in his reactions.

TIMID OR FEARFUL

A really timid puppy shows signs like those of a shy puppy, but in an exaggerated form.

WHAT YOU SEE
The puppy may be reluctant to come to you, may grovel submissively or pee when you pay him attention. An extremely timid puppy may even run or hide from you.

WHAT TO DO
As with the shy puppy, give this pup plenty of time to come to you, and don't move toward him or make eye contact until he's happy to approach. Play with a toy or some small treats to tempt him to engage. See if his shyness diminishes when you're gently interacting with him.

WHAT IT MIGHT INDICATE
A really fearful puppy needs plenty of patience and surroundings that are not too varied or busy to thrive. He will need plenty of positive encouragement in training, and will probably do best with his key person around for most of the time.

No. 5 PUPPY PROOFING YOUR HOME

PREVENTION AND SAFETY

*P*ups are inquisitive and will eat, sniff out, and chew on whatever arouses their curiosity. As a responsible pet parent, it's your job to walk through your home looking at it from the eyes of a puppy, so that you can remove dangers and keep your pup safe.

BEHIND THE SIGNS

What My Pup's Behavior Says

Changes in energy or appetite, diarrhea, lethargy, vomiting, and staggering movements are all indications your pup may have ingested something he shouldn't have. He may be fine once he gets it out of his system, or he may need immediate medical assistance. There are many factors involved, including what and how much was ingested, and the pup's age, size, and health. If you are unsure, err on the safe side and contact your veterinarian or the nearest emergency animal clinic immediately.

POISONOUS PLANTS

Nibbling on a spider plant's leaves can lead to vomiting, and eating even one mistletoe berry can be fatal. The chart in this chapter has more on plants to watch out for, and your veterinarian can provide information specific to the area in which you live.

TOXIC SUBSTANCES

Keep garage and tool shed doors closed and locked to prevent your pup getting in, and place all dangerous items, such as paint thinner, barbeque lighter fluid, insecticides, and antifreeze, on high shelves as an added precaution.

Antifreeze is especially dangerous because it smells good and tastes sweet to pups, so they'll be tempted to lick up the drips from a car's radiator or drink from toilet bowls and outdoor water fountains that have been winterized with the substance. Kidney failure may result, even from just one tablespoon of antifreeze.

Symptoms of antifreeze poisoning are not always easy to spot but include unsteadiness, drooling, vomiting, and excessive thirst. Veterinarian treatment can be lifesaving if administered within the first 8–12 hours.

To lower the risk of antifreeze poisoning choose a brand that contains a bittering agent, meant to make antifreeze less appealing to animals. Look for antifreeze with propylene glycol as an ingredient (instead of the very poisonous ethylene glycol, used in many brands). They are still toxic, but to a lesser degree.

GARBAGE CAN

To most pups the trash can is a treasure trove, a trait their human families find increasingly frustrating as they clean up scattered garbage from the floor. Even worse than the mess, our pups can get quite ill if they eat something they shouldn't, such as chocolate, onions, or chicken bones.

Training can help keep their noses clean, but for some pups the garbage can is always going to be a temptation. The canine sense of smell is one reason why. It's 10,000–100,000 times as acute as our own, making trash—especially food scraps—irresistible to curious pups. Making it inaccessible is your best bet.

Keep it behind a closed door, perhaps one that uses a childproof latch so that your pup can't open it. Or use a bungee cord to secure the lid to the can. A heavy type that uses a foot pedal to open the lid can also be a deterrent.

ELECTRICAL CORDS

Chewing on wires is a common behavior because pups are naturally curious animals who explore with their mouths. Plus, when they're teething it's a practice that feels good. It's also destructive and can be dangerous.
- Hide cords behind furniture, or under the carpet.
- Cover cords with plastic tubing.
- Provide lots of chew toy alternatives.
- Use a pet deterrent spray on the cords that will make them taste bad.

DANGEROUS ITEMS
- Sewing and craft supplies, from buttons to string.
- Office supplies—for example, paper clips and rubber bands.
- Medication, cotton balls, razors.
- Plastic bags.
- Board game pieces and small kids toys.

SAFE PRACTICES
- Keep toilet lids closed, so small puppies can't fall in.
- Washing machine and dryer doors should never be left open (a warm dryer can seem like a cozy place for a nap).

- Screen doors should be latched and windows should be screened.
- Yard and pool fences should be high enough to prevent your pup from jumping over.

Puppy proofing is about keeping your pup safe from dangers—and also keeping your possessions safe from your pup:

- Move any breakables that can be knocked over (for example, that vase on your coffee table).
- Keep shoes in your closet with the door closed to prevent your closet becoming a toy chest full of chew toys for your pup.
- Make sure there are no dangling drape cords that a playful pup can pull down.

POISONOUS PLANTS

Most people are surprised that so many plants pose a danger to canines. If the plant is ingested your pup may suffer temporarily—for example, by vomiting to rid himself of the toxins. Sometimes, however, the effects can be much more serious and even life-threatening. Luckily, many pups will show no interest in these plants. For those that do, contact your veterinarian immediately. This list is not exhaustive, but includes many of the most dangerous plants.

	SYMPTOMS
Amaryllis bulbs	Changes in energy level, diarrhea, excessive saliva, tremors, upset stomach
Azalea	Difficulty breathing, lethargy, upset stomach, vomiting
Castor bean	Abdominal pain, dehydration, diarrhea, drooling, excessive thirst, lethargy, loss of appetite, muscle twitching, seizures, vomiting
Cherry tree and shrubs	Difficulty breathing, dilated pupils, overexcitement, exhaustion
Chrysanthemum	Allergic reaction (dermatitis)—itchy or inflamed skin, diarrhea, drooling, vomiting
Daffodil bulbs	Allergic reaction (dermatitis)—itchy or inflamed skin; gastrointestinal irritation—vomiting, diarrhea
English ivy	Allergic reaction (dermatitis)—itchy or inflamed skin; diarrhea, drooling, upset stomach, vomiting

	SYMPTOMS
Foxglove	Gastrointestinal irritation—upset stomach, vomiting
Larkspur	Allergic reaction (dermatitis)—itchy or inflamed skin; upset stomach
Mistletoe berries	Allergic reaction (dermatitis)—itchy or inflamed skin; changes in appetite, diarrhea, vomiting, weakness
Oleander	Allergic reaction (dermatitis)—itchy or inflamed skin; digestive problems—diarrhea, vomiting; heart problems
Onion	Anaemia—lethargy, pale gums (loss of the normal pink color)
Ragwort	Irreversible kidney failure and liver damage
Rhododendron	Allergic reaction (dermatitis)—itchy or inflamed skin; upset stomach
Rhubarb leaves	Tremors, seizures
Spider plant	Drooling, vomiting
Tulip (Narcissus) bulbs	Changes in appetite, diarrhea, heart problems, skin irritation, vomiting, weakness, tremors, seizures
Yew	Dilated pupils, disorientation, abdominal pain, vomiting, cardiac failure

EYES IN THE BACK OF YOUR HEAD

While it's easy to read a list of what to do and not to do when you're puppy proofing, if it's been a while since you had a puppy (or if this one is your first), it'll come as a surprise quite how enterprising your new pet can be when it comes to getting hold of things that he shouldn't.

Scan all rooms before your pup moves in and answer these questions:

- What's on the floor? Anything other than permitted toys or puppy pads needs to be moved up high. Shoes with their intriguingly "human" smell tend to be particularly attractive and even the first set of small-but-sharp puppy teeth can usually get through leather in minutes. Don't just unplug cables, put them out of reach. This might be the time to invest in a rubber cable-holder; you wind cables onto these and contain them in a heavy rubber cover which would be a challenge for even sharp puppy teeth to penetrate.

- What's on the level above the floor? Just because the coffee table is above puppy eye level, don't assume it's inaccessible. Inquisitive puppies can have impressive scrambling ability. Any remotes, tablets, phones, or even shreddable magazines or books should be up high ("high" may be higher than you think). Remotes have a particular appeal because people constantly handle them so they smell appetizingly human. And they don't take long to crunch into little pieces, so make sure all of yours are out of reach.

- Have you pushed the chairs in under the table? Otherwise chairs or stools left "out" can offer a handy stepladder to an inquisitive puppy, and once he's on a highish table, he's a danger to himself as well as to your possessions. The same is true for stools or boxes next to worktops.

- Are there any purses or school bags, or anything else, lying around? Check not just for things on the floor but also for items laid on chairs or even hanging from hooks. Bags make great exploring games for puppies—they hold a whole range of things, from pill packs and spectacles to change purses. By all means make a safe game for him by hiding treats in a fabric bag, but don't leave your own around for him to "discover."

- What about soft furnishings? If he's still at the housebreaking, accident-prone stage, it may be best to put an old

OPTIONAL SUPPLIES

Baby gate

If you want to keep your pup in one room temporarily, a baby gate may be the answer. Look for one that he can't slide under, and with bars close enough together so that he can't get his head stuck. If your pup likes to gnaw on the furniture avoid wooden gates.

Coats or sweaters

Winter wear for your puppy is more than a fashion statement—it's insulation. He'll need it if he'll be spending much time in cold weather, especially if he is a small breed or a short-haired pup.

Crate

The crate has three main purposes:
1. To contain your pup when traveling.
2. To provide a sleeping area for your pup at home.
3. Housetraining, since pups don't like to soil where they sleep.

Puppies are den animals; a crate provides a secure and cozy space that's all their own to curl up in. It's not to be used for long-term confinement or for punishment.

Look for a crate that is easy to clean (such as wire or plastic). It should be big enough for your pup to stand up and turn around, but not much more. If you get a larger crate and your pup is not yet housetrained, you may want to consider a divider that will make the space smaller.

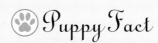

Puppy Fact

Squeaky toys can pose a danger for the curious pup, as he could chew through the toy to find what is making the noise and then ingest it. Some rawhide chew toys can be a choking hazard. Any chew toy that is small enough to be swallowed should be kept away from your pup.

This can help prevent a pup from using one part of the crate to sleep and the other part as a potty area. If there's only room to sleep, it's unlikely he will eliminate there.

Exercise pen

Similar to a child's playpen, an exercise pen is useful if you need to keep your pup contained in a small area, but with more room to play and move around than his crate offers.

Treats

They're a great way to reward your pup and reinforce behavior. Small bite-sized treats work best for this, in whatever flavor your pup prefers.

THE FIRST DAY AND NIGHT

he day you bring your puppy home has finally arrived. It's a happy day for you, but for your pup it can be a confusing, and slightly scary, experience. In a few days he'll have settled in, but until then your home is full of strange sights, sounds, and smells. Different may be exciting for your pup, but it can also be stressful.

Early associations stick, so you want to make day one as calm and comforting as possible. Above all, be gentle and patient with your puppy during his first days with you. Don't scold or speak harshly to him, even if he is destructive or makes a mess. In his confused state, that may only make him fear you. This initiation period should be an enjoyable time in which you set the tone of your relationship, your puppy learns to trust you, and you form the basis for a happy life together.

BEFORE PICKING YOUR PUP UP

Plan to bring your puppy home on a long weekend, or when you have three or four days where you can stay with him and get him settled. Mornings are the best time to bring him home, so he has time to explore, feed, play, and tire himself out before bedtime.

Avoid bringing your pup home during a holiday celebration or when you have guests. It can be too much for your pup to take in at once, plus your puppy needs all of your attention at this time.

Puppy proof your home in advance (see chapter 5) and ask the shelter or the breeder not to feed your pup for at least an hour before you arrive to pick him up. It can help prevent carsickness on the way home. Find out ahead of time if your pup has a favorite blanket that can accompany him on the car ride, as it may

provide some comfort. Decide on a quiet and cozy (but not isolated) area for your pup to sleep, and get his bed or crate ready. Having your puppy share your bed is not advised, as it can lead to behavioral problems.

Choose the command words you'll use with your pup to let him know it's time to eliminate, or time to sleep. Make sure everyone in your home knows what the words are, so you can all use them from the start. Consistency is key. It will put you and your puppy on the path to understanding each other. Make an appointment for your puppy to have a health check with a veterinarian. Schedule it for a few days after your puppy is home.

The Name Game

CHOOSING:

Your puppy's name should not sound like any of the command words you will be using to communicate with him. For example, "no" sounds a lot like "Mo," and "stay" sounds a lot like "May." It will only cause confusion. One- or two-syllable names are easiest for your pup to understand.

TEACHING:

Whenever your pup looks at you say his name happily. He'll soon make the connection. Reward him with a treat when you call his name and he responds.

PREPARE FOR THE CAR RIDE

Spread some old towels over the seat and floor of the car in case your puppy is sick on the way home. He may not have much experience as a passenger, and the chances are he'll also be nervous. Have a puppy toy available for the drive, as it may provide a distraction for your pup.

If your puppy will be crated, lay a soft covering in the crate to make it more comfortable. Bring along a sheet that can be used to cover the crate, just in case. It may help your pup feel less anxious. You'll need to see what works best for your pup. If he hasn't been crated before, the day you bring your puppy home isn't the right time to start. When you get to the shelter or breeders spend at least 15 minutes playing with your pup there. It will help your pup release some energy before traveling, and give him a chance to feel comfortable with you. Go for a walk before leaving. It may tire your puppy, and it will encourage him to go to the toilet before he gets in the car.

ON THE WAY HOME

Have someone else drive so you can focus on your puppy. He should travel leashed and on your lap, wrapped loosely in a blanket. Or he can travel in a crate—there's plenty of time to get him used to a seatbelt or harness later on. Don't let your pup roam free in the car. It's not safe, and moving around in a vehicle can also make him more prone to carsickness.

Your puppy may cry or bark and that's normal. It's an unfamiliar day for him. Don't try to calm him with extra attention or affection. It will just reinforce the behavior. If you stay calm and don't treat the day as a big deal he will hopefully follow your lead.

If you need to stop to give your pup a bathroom break find an area that doesn't get much foot traffic, especially if your pup has not had all of his puppy vaccinations yet. You don't want to add more people or other animals to an already confusing day, and until your pup has had the necessary shots he needs to stay away from other dogs. If a break isn't necessary then go straight home.

AT HOME ON DAY ONE
Keep your puppy on his leash during his first introduction to your home. Before going inside, walk your pup to the area you've chosen for him to use to relieve himself. Give him the command word you've chosen to use for this activity, such as "go potty", and some time to eliminate, and praise him if he does.

Enter your home, with your pup following behind you. You want to send the message from the start that you are the pack leader.

Family members or other pets should stay out of sight until your pup's had a chance to explore his new home and is feeling less anxious.

Introduce your pup to just one room first, the room where his food and water is. He should feel more comfortable once he's eaten. Make sure it's the same food he's used to. There are too many other changes for your puppy to deal with at this time. Switching his food without a gradual transition to the new food can also cause digestive issues. Slowly introduce your pup to other rooms, giving him a chance to sniff and explore. Avoid any rooms that will be off limits.

Once your puppy has seen his new home you can invite family members into the room one at a time. They should pay no attention to the pup until he approaches them without being coaxed, at which time they can praise him and give him a treat. It's important that your pup comes to them, at his own pace.

SEND YOUR PUPPY A MESSAGE

To follow the rules of your home your pup must first know what they are.

When your pup behaves badly give him a stern "no" and then ignore him. It will teach him not to repeat the behavior. Only good behavior should get rewarded with attention.

Start the way you mean to proceed. That means, for example, no to having your pup sleep in your bed, even at first.

Use commands, such as "sit" and "stay" from the beginning. Day one is not the time to start training exercises (officially, that is) but it is the time to form the habits that will help you and your puppy understand each other.

Puppy Fact

Be prepared for accidents in the home, even if your pup comes to you fully housetrained. He may be anxious or excited, which can cause him to temporarily forget his training.

Take your puppy outside for a potty break every hour or two, and after naps and meals. Give him a bit of time and if he doesn't eliminate bring him back outside every 15 minutes or so to try again. Expect accidents, but praise him when he does eliminate in the designated spot. If your backyard is not securely fenced, use the leash each time you take your puppy out. Keep a record of when your puppy relieves himself. This will help you get to know his schedule, and anticipate when he needs to go out.

Home rules should go into effect from the very start. You may be tempted to hold off until your pup is settled, but it's more confusing for your pup if he's allowed to do something at the beginning (like sleeping in your bed) and then not allowed to do it later.

Why Your Pup Can't Sleep

The first couple of nights are usually difficult. There is a chance your pup may be so tired out from the day that he'll sleep soundly, but more often there is an adjustment period. It may be the first time your pup is away from his littermates and he may be missing them, or the familiarity of the breeder's home or the shelter.

You'll have plenty of people who want to come by and see your new puppy. Have them wait at least three days, and then have only one or two visitors at a time. Too many people too soon can overwhelm your pup and make it harder for him to feel at home.

Leave the first three or four days with your new puppy open, so that you can focus on him. This is an important bonding time. Try to spend most of your day in the same room with your puppy —even during periods when you're not interacting with him—so he can see you. When he wants to play with you, join in.

THE FIRST NIGHT

Puppies nap a lot, but try to prevent it within two hours of bedtime. Play with your pup before bedtime, to help tire him out. Take your pup outside just before lights out, and wait for him to eliminate. (Don't forget to praise him when he does, as this is behavior you want to encourage.)

Lead your pup to his bed in the kitchen, den or wherever you have decided is best. Close the doors to the room so he can't roam the house. If using a crate, don't expect your puppy to take to the crate right away, especially if he hasn't used one before. Leave the doors to the crate open for the first couple of nights, until he feels safe in it. Make sure there are some blankets and a chew toy in the crate to make it inviting.

Your puppy will probably be restless and whimper when he's left alone. To help him feel less lonely put an article of clothing that has your scent on it in his bed (like a T-shirt). Leaving a radio on low can also help. A few chew toys may help distract him. Check on your pup every few hours to see if he needs to go out, but don't wake him if he's asleep.

Try to ignore any whimpering, hard as it

🐾 Puppy Fact

Too much stimulation can make it more difficult for your pup to settle in. During his first couple of days he may need short periods of time where he can be alone but can still see you (for example, through a baby gate).

may be. Cuddling and reassuring your pup will just encourage him to continue the behavior. It teaches your puppy that when he acts a certain way he gets your attention. Although it seems mean it's really for the best that you don't give in, and it will help him settle into the right routine sooner. (Do check on him regularly though. Maybe he's crying because he needs to go out, and not because he wants your attention.) Your pup will be up early in the morning and so will you, so you can let him out to eliminate first thing.

OTHER PETS

Don't deprive established pets of your attention, or they may become jealous of the new puppy.

Introduce your puppy to other pets in the home gradually. Start out using baby gates to keep them separated, so they can see, smell, and get used to each other. (If your pup is small enough to slide underneath you may want to look at gates made specifically for dogs.) When they are comfortable you can remove the gates, but your pets will need supervision as they get to know one another. This is the case even if the other pet is another dog. They may both speak canine, but until they establish their roles communication between them may not be positive.

Never leave your new puppy alone with your other pets. Feed them separately until they have become friends.

Settling In

After a day and a night spent tending to your puppy, you may find yourself wondering whether you have the time for a pet after all. Don't worry—you're both at the adjustment stage; provided that you give him a schedule and stick to it, and are careful to follow a timetable for his housetraining, you'll find that he'll fit in with your life just fine—but it will take him a week or two to settle in. And you'll become accustomed to fitting around his needs, too.

No. 8 A MEAL FIT FOR A PUPPY

WHAT AND WHEN TO FEED

sk the shelter or breeder what food your pup is currently eating, how much, and on what schedule. Continue this schedule, at least at first—it can help your pup adjust more easily to his new home, especially given all the other changes he'll be experiencing.

DRY OR WET FOOD?

Dry food (also known as "kibble") can promote dental health, and it can encourage a dog to slow down and chew his food, instead of gobbling it up quickly. It's easy to store, and to measure out portions. Wet food may help ease digestive problems. It may be the better option for pups with dental issues that make chewing painful. Whichever option you choose, most important is making sure that the food you feed your pup meets his daily needs.

DIETARY REQUIREMENTS

The food we eat makes a difference in how we feel and our overall health. The same is true for the food your pup eats.

Choose a food formulated for puppies, as they have specific dietary requirements. It should contain 20–25 percent protein (preferably a meat protein, for example chicken or beef) to meet the particular energy needs of a puppy. It should also contain fats, carbohydrates (such as oats, barley, or rice), and vitamins and minerals. The low-end puppy food brands may be less expensive but a pup generally needs more of this food to meet his daily needs— which could be met with a smaller portion of a higher-quality brand. Directions on the food packaging are a recommendation only. Your veterinarian can tell you if your pup would benefit from less or more food.

MEAL VARIETY

For most people the idea of having the same food at each meal would not be appealing. It's not the same with dogs. Your pup will not be bored of his food, although the occasional treat is always welcome. In fact, changing foods can be bad for his digestion.

FREE OR SCHEDULED FEEDING?

Leaving a food bowl out so that your pup can eat from it whenever he wants is known as "free feeding." Scheduled feeding is when you feed your pup at set times each day, removing the bowl after about 20 minutes. Scheduled feeding is preferrable because:

1. It makes housetraining easier. When a pup eats can help you predict when he will need to relieve himself (usually about 20–30 minutes after eating).

2. It can help your pup understand there is a specific time for each activity. When his food bowl goes down it's time to eat.

3. It makes it easier to control your pup's food intake. Free feeding can lead to overeating. This can cause a pup to grow too rapidly, and bone growth disease may result.

4. It allows you to identify changes in your pup's eating patterns. A loss of appetite can be a sign of illness.

HOW OFTEN TO FEED YOUR PUP

These are general guidelines. Your veterinarian should be consulted to establish what your pup's needs are, based on age, breed, size, and health.

PUPPY FEEDING CHART

Under eight weeks	During this time a pup receives much of his nourishment from his mother's milk, complemented by solid food starting at around three weeks of age.
Under six months of age	Most pups do well with two to four meals per day, depending on their individual requirements. An example of pups who may require up to four meals per day would be smaller breeds (for example: Bichon Frise, Cavalier King, Pomeranian, Toy Spaniel, and more), as they can suffer from low blood sugar (hypoglycaemia).
Over six months of age	Two meals per day for most pups, or as advised by your veterinarian.

What Your Pup's Stool Is Telling You

Firm, dark brown stools are a sign of good digestion. Soft or light colored stools are a sign of a problem with diet or digestion. Loose stools are a sign of overfeeding.

SKIPPING MEALS

If your puppy avoids his food for a meal or two it's not usually a problem, but watch him carefully. Does he seem lethargic, have stomach issues, or seem in any way distressed? If so, contact your veterinarian.

TREAT DISPENSING/FOOD TOYS

You fill the toy with dry puppy food, and your pup then has to solve the puzzle of the toy to have the food released. There are a variety of options on the market, and they are a great way to keep your pup occupied and exercise his mind. They're especially useful if you will be out of the house at a time when your pup would normally be fed. Your pup won't miss a meal—he'll just have to work for it, and the food toy will keep him happily busy.

FEEDING TIPS

- Always leave water out and easy available to your pup.
- Set your pup's food out at the same time you sit down to your own meal. It sets a routine, and makes your pup feel included in your mealtimes.
- Place your pup's food bowl in his crate

How to Change Your Pup's Food

Transitioning to a new food too quickly can result in an upset stomach and diarrhea. Make the change gradually over the course of a week to prevent this. Start out with about 20 percent new food and 80 percent old food on day one. From there increase the amount of new food, while decreasing the amount of old food each day. By the end of the week your pup should be only eating the new food.

to help him associate the crate with comfort.

- Don't feed your pup from your plate or make a habit of giving him people food.
- Don't try to remove your pup's bowl or interrupt him while he is eating. It can cause some pups to react aggressively.
- Remove anything that's left in your pup's food bowl after 20 to 30 minutes of setting his dish down. If your pup has walked away from his bowl without finishing it may be because the portions are too large.
- Don't feed your pup an hour before or after exercising him (a walk is fine, but a run or vigorous game of catch should be avoided).
- Avoid feeding your pup an hour before car travel.
- Make any changes to your pup's food gradually, to help him adjust to the new food.
- If your pup is not used to dry food and that's what you'd like him to eat try adding a bit of water to it at the beginning.

FUSSY EATERS

If your pup seems like a fussy eater it may really mean that the portions he's being fed are too large, he's been given too many treats, or he's being fed people food (for example, from the table). If you try to tempt your pup to eat he may learn to enjoy that attention, more than the food in his bowl.

Here's what to do: cut down on the treats, make sure no one is giving the pup people food and stop trying to coax him to eat. Stick with scheduled feedings and remove the food bowl after 20 or so minutes, even if food remains. Don't feed your pup until his next regular meal. Chances are, you'll find he's not a fussy eater at all.

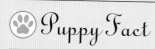

Puppy Fact

Treats should never make up more than 5 percent of your pup's daily food intake.

TREATS

Many owners give their puppies the occasional small treat of human food. While this may be harmless as an indulgence, make sure it isn't too often, and never feed your puppy from the table—you don't want him becoming a pest during meals. A handful of foods are harmful to dogs and should never be given. If your puppy eats any of them accidentally, consult your vet immediately.

RAW FEEDING

There's an increasing trend toward feeding dogs raw food, usually known as the BARF (Bones and Raw Food) or Raw diets. These consist either of raw meat and bones only, or of meat mixed with vegetables and ground bone. There are arguments both for and against; arguments for claim that raw is the most natural and the healthiest way to feed a dog (and that puppies can be fed raw directly from the point that they are weaned), that it fits the way a dog's digestion works better than cooked food, and that it's a way of avoiding the additives that are in nearly all commercial pet food. Those less keen believe that raw meat and bones can contain bacteria that would be eliminated by the high-temperature cooking that is part of the commercial food process, and that can make your puppy sick. If you're interested in feeding your puppy raw, check with your veterinarian and make sure that you buy food from a reputable supplier.

CHEWING

All puppies need to chew—almost constantly at some stages in their development. Your pup won't see any difference between what he's allowed to chew and what he isn't, so it's up to you to keep him supplied with what he needs, and to keep the things he *shouldn't* chew out of harm's way.

FOODS YOUR DOG SHOULDN'T EAT

AVOCADO
Contains persin, which can be toxic to dogs in large quantities.

CHOCOLATE AND COCOA PRODUCTS
These contain theobromine, an alkaloid that dogs can't process and that can poison them. The dog chocolate treats that are sold in pet shops don't contain any cocoa so are safe to feed. Some chocolate products also contain caffeine, which is toxic to dogs.

GRAPES AND RAISINS
These can cause kidney failure in dogs. The reason isn't known. Dogs have been seen to eat grapes or raisins without ill effects on one occasion, then become very ill on another. Avoid altogether.

GARLIC AND ONIONS
Eaten in quantity, and particularly raw, both can affect a dog's red blood cells, leading to anaemia.

MACADAMIA NUTS
Although the reason isn't known, macadamia nuts can cause tremors and weakness in a dog's muscle system, and provoke a fever.

XYLITOL
An artificial sweetener that is used in low-sugar or sugar-free cakes and cookies, and is also an ingredient in sugar-free gum. Eaten in any quantity it provokes an abrupt drop in blood sugar levels and can cause seizures in dogs.

STAGES OF CHEWING

Puppies go through three distinct chewing stages, and most dogs enjoy chewing all their lives: it's a natural activity for them.

The first stage is when a pup's needle-sharp milk teeth come through—at around three weeks, often prompting the mother dog to begin weaning her litter. By the time you bring him home, at around eight weeks, your puppy will have a full set of milk teeth. At this age, although a puppy will chew anything, his jaw strength is not developed and he will do considerably less damage with his teeth than becomes possible later, when his adult teeth come through.

The second stage is while his adult teeth are developing, starting at around four months. Puppies of this age will chew perpetually, partly to sooth their aching gums as they teethe. By the time your dog is eight months old, he will have all 42 adult teeth.

The third stage is adolescent chewing—it tends to last for around six months,

Puppy Fact

Chewing is enjoyable and satisfying for dogs; they have a set of complex muscles around their cheeks and jaws, some of which are only exercised by chewing.

from eight to 14 months. It is less well understood than the earlier, teething stage but behaviorists think that it reflects the dog's urge to explore the world around him and experiment with new experiences.

From around 14 months, your dog is a young adult and although most dogs will get lifelong pleasure from chewing a meaty bone or a rawhide, the extreme, incessant chewing of the puppy stage is usually over.

WHAT HE CAN CHEW

You'd prefer your puppy didn't chew your shoes or the TV remote, so lay in a supply of things he can chew, and put anything he shouldn't be chewing away or out of reach. For his safety, puppy-proof leads and wires: they can look strongly appealing to a teething puppy. Alternate chew toys daily to keep him interested. Try some or all of the following:

- Rawhide chews: These are available in various sizes, from thin twists or strips suitable for small puppies to larger hide "cigars" or knotted shapes that will last longer with slightly older pups.
- Nylon bones: Durable, almost indestructible, and available in a variety of sizes.
- Hollow rubber toys: These can be stuffed with flavored pastes or small biscuits, and can engage a puppy for a while as he exercises his jaws and tries to get the food out. For a puppy who is teething, try stuffing the toy and then placing it in the freezer for an hour or two before giving it to him: the cold will soothe his sore gums, and it will take him longer to get the food out, too.
- Sterilized bones: Hollow marrow bones can be stuffed with food in the same way as rubber toys.
- Cardboard tubes or empty boxes can make good chewing toys for small puppies. Place a few small treats in an empty cardboard box to make an impromptu hide-and-go-seek game.

BEHIND THE SIGNS

Your Puppy's Teeth

Like people, dogs have two sets of teeth—the baby or milk set come through at around three weeks and consist of 28 needle-sharp teeth; they begin to be displaced at about four months, when the puppy starts to develop the second, adult, set—42 teeth that have usually come in fully by the time the puppy is around eight months old.

THE POWER OF POSITIVE EXPERIENCES

*S*ocialization describes the experience of gently exposing your pup to new experiences and the world around him, so that he finds the normal encounters and ups and downs of everyday life easy and comfortable to cope with.

The Learning Window

Dog behaviorists sometimes refer to the puppy "learning" or "imprinting" window. This applies to puppies from birth to 16 weeks old—the time at which a pup's brain is absorbing information and learning about life at a tremendously fast rate and he's picking things up more quickly than he ever will again. Lessons learned during this time tend to be learned for life, so it's important that a puppy's early experiences are positive ones.

While it may not be possible to introduce your puppy to all the life experiences he may have in just his first few weeks with you, the more new and positive experiences he has as a puppy, the more likely he is to understand that "new" doesn't have to mean threatening, and to take the unexpected in his stride.

WHY SOCIALIZE?

A well-socialized pup will grow up to be a happy and confident dog. He won't see the world as a frightening place, or be resistant to, or fearful about, change. He'll adapt to different circumstances more easily, expect the best from new encounters and make for a well-adjusted pet and companion.

If a puppy isn't socialized carefully, he's more likely to have problems with new experiences, people, and other dogs, and may react fearfully to change. As fear can easily translate into aggression in an older dog, good socialization is vital in your pet's journey to a well-balanced adulthood.

TIMING FOR SOCIALIZATION

For their first two years, dogs are constantly learning and absorbing new information (and, despite the saying, you can teach an old dog new tricks—it simply takes longer, and certain lessons learned in puppyhood are hard to change once the dog is an adult). The first six months, though, are crucial for learning,

and the first 16 weeks of a dog's life are the most important of all. As you probably brought your puppy home at eight weeks, this means that his socialization in the first two months that you have him should be carefully planned.

SETTING YOUR PUPPY UP FOR SUCCESS

You can't control everything about your puppy's encounters with the outside world. You can set yourself up for success, though, by preplanning a lot of his first experiences. For example, you can line up other owners with older dogs who you know to be friendly and calm for your pup to mix with, and arrange for your puppy to meet and play with a dog-savvy child who has previous experience with puppies and who won't be too rough or overexcitable with him. Read through the whole chapter and think about all the activities and exercises, then plan ahead to ensure that your puppy has mostly positive and nonthreatening experiences during this vital time in his development. The reward will be his growing confidence as he encounters the new and the unfamiliar.

YOUR PUPPY'S CHARACTER

Every puppy is an individual: he may have traits characteristic of his breed, but he's still unique. This means that you can't treat socialization as a cookie-cutter exercise, and that your pet will reach milestones at his own rate. Some puppies bound into new experiences enthusiastically and with few fears, while others are cautious and take longer to adjust. And still others, probably the majority, show mixed responses, finding some novelties easier to cope with than others. To be successful, socialization must follow your puppy's natural pace.

ACTING AS PACK LEADER

You are your pup's filter for new experiences, and he should look to you for guidance when he's unsure. Remember that how you behave affects how he sees things; most dogs pick up the body language of both other dogs and people with incredible speed. When you're organizing a new experience for your pet, approach it confidently and cheerfully; he'll be guided by your cues.

WHAT IF THINGS DON'T WORK OUT?

It's hard to stage-manage everything, and sometimes something unplanned may upset or scare your puppy. For example, a child may reach down and "pet" him roughly before you have time to intervene. Afterward, he may back away from children or try to hide behind your legs. When an introduction doesn't go to plan, take a step or two backward and recreate the experience, but managed by you—get a child to throw treats near your puppy but without touching him, for example, or to sit on the floor near him but without moving toward him, giving him time to approach her. It may take several positive experiences to win out over the negative one.

BE CONSISTENT

Your puppy is learning 24 hours a day—not just at the moments when you are consciously introducing him to new things. Whatever you are doing counts—if you're vacuuming, for example, make sure that your puppy has seen the vacuum, heard the noise it makes, and doesn't seem too perturbed before you vacuum the whole house. If you can't manage an experience, have a friend remove your puppy from it until you can.

VACCINATION AND SOCIALIZATION

In the past, vet advice was usually to recommend that owners keep their new puppy at home until he had had all his shots. Since vaccinations are given at least twice, when the puppy is six and twelve weeks old, and sometimes a third shot is offered at four months, this would mean that the puppy's socialization was limited to experiences at home during the key imprinting window of development. Today, vets generally recommend that you take your pet out and about at a younger age (you can carry him in areas that may be riskier for him, for example heavy dog-traffic areas such as the local dog park), but with some caution, and especially avoid him mixing with dogs if you don't know that they have been vaccinated. It's a judged risk: ask your own vet's advice, as they will know if there are any specific health threats in your local area, and will probably also recommend that your puppy is vaccinated as early as possible.

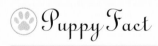

Puppy Fact

Your puppy's body language will tell you how he's feeling about new things—if he tucks his tail, or starts sniffing the ground around him even though he's just had a pee break, he's letting you know he's feeling anxious.

STARTING SOCIALIZATION EXERCISES

At home

Begin socialization as soon as you bring your puppy home. Set yourself some goals and remember that, in the house, distraction often works well. Attach a leash to your puppy's collar but leave it trailing: that way, you can pick it up to hold him back—for example, from the front door, or from bouncing at the vacuum cleaner—while you're going through various exercises at home.

Dealing with machines

Keep plenty of small but tasty treats in your pocket, so that you can distract your puppy with something tempting if he shows any kind of apprehensive reaction. As usual, timing is key: you need to offer the treat at the precise moment the dishwasher starts its rumbling cycle (or any other noise starts). Take things slowly, at your puppy's own pace.

Two people and a very gradual approach may be needed for some exercises. The vacuum, which both roars and moves, is often very alarming for puppies. If you try to see it through your puppy's eyes, it's an unpredictable, huge monster that moves jerkily round the house—so it's hardly surprising that it worries him. Try acclimatizing your puppy in a number of stages: first take the vacuum out of the cupboard and let it sit in the living room, offering your puppy a treat while he looks at it. Leave it out, and next day, have someone switch it on for just two or three seconds—no longer—again offering a treat. Have your puppy on a leash so that he can't fly over and attack it, but if he tries to move away from it, let him retreat to a distance he's comfortable with. Leave a gap of a few hours before switching it on again, and again, leave it on for just a few seconds. Treat your puppy. If he bounces and barks, wait until he's calm before offering a treat. This system works for most unexpected noises in the house, and can be extended to noises outside.

Meeting children

It's crucial that your puppy learns not to be afraid of children, or be snappy with them. A puppy may find the high-pitched noises and sudden movements that children make intimidating, or may get overexcited playing with children, if he isn't used to them. Make sure that the child or children he's being introduced to understand that the puppy may find them frightening, and they know that they shouldn't surround him, or go after him if he backs off. Give them some treats and ask them to scatter them around their feet at first until the puppy approaches them on his own. If he is happy to be pet, encourage them to stroke him gently on his sides or under his chin, rather than grabbing at him, or holding his face.

AIMS OF SOCIALIZATION

A well-socialized young dog will be able to:

- Cope with being calmly handled by a familiar person, and having his paws, mouth, and ears looked at without becoming overly apprehensive.
- Accept being handled and examined at the vet's surgery.
- Manage polite introductions to other puppies and adult dogs.
- Meet and greet new people in a friendly way, out and about or in the house—and particularly at the front door—without undue caution or overexuberant barking and jumping.
- Cope with a range of noises in the house—for example, the doorbell, vacuum cleaner, hairdryer, and dishwasher—without overreacting or going on the defensive.
- Cope with a range of noises outside the house—for example,

ambulance or police sirens, heavy traffic, the garbage truck, at a construction site, and at a train or subway station.
- Deal with crowds in outside spaces—for example, at the farmers' market, the shopping mall, or the skateboard park.
- See other animals without becoming too excited or unmanageable (this will vary according to where you live: in the country, a puppy should become familiar with livestock such as sheep, cows, and horses; this is less important in town). It may be impossible to socialize every dog successfully with cats—sometimes a puppy's prey drive is too great—but the younger your puppy is when he first meets or mixes with a cat, the higher the likelihood is that they will settle together.

Encounters with children should always be supervized; it may not be possible to teach the under-10s to be consistent or appropriate in their approach to a puppy, and if you're not on hand to manage play, your puppy may feel forced to protect himself against rough handling or overstimulating play. Never, ever leave a puppy alone with young children. In time, they can learn to be good friends, but this depends on plenty of positive early interaction. If he is going to live with children, get them together for "calm time" a couple of times a day; if he isn't, arrange for him to have controlled meetings with children twice a week.

At the front door

The front door is an exciting place for your puppy. It's where arrivals and departures take place, and all the bustle of the household happens. You need to teach him to greet visitors pleasantly but without over-the-top excitement. Stage-manage your puppy's first front-door meetings—get friends or family members to ring the doorbell, and have someone hold your puppy's leash and encourage him to stand back as you open the door. If he's learning the "sit" command, this is a good time to use it. Praise and treat him for calm greetings and make sure that your "visitors" are armed with treats for these first encounters. Ignore any jumping or barking, and only treat him and allow him to greet visitors once he is calm.

Outside
Meeting other dogs

Make sure that you know the first other adult dogs your puppy encounters, and that they're calm and likely to be tolerant of puppy manners. Try to introduce them outside, and have both dogs on their leads at first—the backyard is ideal, as, if the meeting goes well, they can then be freed to play together. If your puppy is keen to meet the other dog, let him approach freely. The dogs will probably sniff one another, and a shy puppy may lie down, roll over, or lick the adult dog's mouth, which is a submissive sign. If he seems overly fearful, let him take his time approaching and make sure the other dog can't go near him until he is ready. A bold puppy may approach an adult dog by running around it excitedly, or even nipping at its ankles, and an adult dog may use a paw to roll him over, or offer a low growl or curl a lip to send a message that his rowdiness is unacceptable. If the other dog has a good temperament there shouldn't be cause for worry: an adult dog can start to teach him good canine manners without him coming to any harm. Introduce your pup to several dogs individually before you try him in a group: a shy puppy may be overwhelmed by too many dog introductions at once.

Puppy parties

Ask your vet if their surgery holds puppy parties or if they know of any nearby. These are simply meet-and-greet sessions for young dogs. Most puppies love them; it's a chance for rough and tumble with youngsters their own age, and, just like human kindergarten, you'll often find that your pup will make special friends there and you can fix him up with play dates. A puppy may find them overwhelming; keep an eye out and take your puppy away if he seems frightened, or unwilling to be drawn into play.

First vet visit

Arrange your first visit at a quiet time of day when there won't be too many other animals in the surgery. Many vets will schedule an introductory visit at which your puppy meets the surgery staff, is made a fuss of, and given treats, so it sets him up with a positive impression for future visits.

Crowded places

Take care taking your puppy into crowds. Carry him for the first one or two experiences and don't overwhelm him: a busy farmers' market or outdoor sports day may have too much noise and fuss for a very young puppy. Keep the trip short (15 minutes is plenty), but repeat it regularly so that he gets used to being in large groups of people gradually.

In the car

Some puppies love the car right away; others get carsick and may drool copiously or actually vomit. The vast majority get over it, and most dogs come to love car journeys, as they represent a visit or a trip to a walk. Keep first journeys short for a few weeks, have someone sit on the back seat with the puppy and keep plenty of old towels on hand to protect against mess. Older puppies should be restrained on the back seat with a special dog seat belt.

TIMETABLE FOR NEW EXPERIENCES

Aim to introduce your puppy to something new, both indoors and outside, a couple of times a week. Take note of those that he copes with easily and others that he seems to find more challenging and vary what you do with him, and how much of it, accordingly. It can help to make a chart of all the things that you want him to get used to and stick it on the refrigerator door to keep a note of what you're practicing with him, and how often.

ℕo. 10 HOUSETRAINING

GETTING IT RIGHT

*I*f you're patient and consistent, housebreaking your puppy won't take very long—many pups get the idea within a couple of weeks, and are able to put it into execution (with the odd lapse) in just another two or three. As his new owner, though, you may find it feels like longer! There are three parts to housetraining speedily and successfully: first, a careful timetable that ensures that your puppy is taken out so regularly that he has the minimum chance of having an accident indoors; second, positive reinforcement, in the form of praise and treats, when he eliminates out of doors, and, third, efficient cleaning up when the inevitable accidents do occur.

BEFORE YOU START

While you're housebreaking your puppy, decide where you're going to allow him to roam freely at home. Accidents are likely to be quite frequent over the first few weeks, so you may opt for just a couple of rooms with hard floors that are easy to clean up. At this stage you can use baby gates—which are easy to put up and take down—to keep your pup from areas you don't want him to go. As he becomes more reliable over the coming weeks, and you no longer have to watch him like a hawk whenever the two of you are indoors, you can gradually enlarge his free space to include carpeted areas and, eventually, give him the run of the house.

PREVENTIVE MEASURES

For the first few weeks, lay down a thick layer of newspaper in the area your puppy spends most of his time. If you lay a sheet of plastic underneath it, it will prevent accidents soaking through, and make them even easier to clean up. However quick on the uptake your puppy is, he's bound to make mistakes for a while.

Puppy training pads are also an option: available at pet shops, these are like flat diapers—made from a highly absorbent top layer backed with a thin plastic sheet that prevents soak-through to the floor underneath. They're convenient to use but relatively expensive—with a young puppy you may find that you're using a lot of them.

HOW CRATE TRAINING CAN HELP

If you're crate training your puppy, it can help to reinforce housetraining. He won't want to make a mess where he sleeps, so will try to avoid accidents when he's confined to his crate. The same will usually hold if you are using a puppy pen for brief periods. Keep your expectations quite low, though—even if he is doing his best, a small puppy's bladder control is not strong. If you've reached the point in crate training where he's shut in for brief periods, keep them short and if he does have an accident, clean up after him as below, without reacting with any scolding or displeasure.

HOW LONG WILL IT TAKE?

Getting your puppy to the point at which he is reliably housetrained varies. If you follow the steps carefully, most puppies will be clean indoors, with the occasional accident, by around four months, and pretty much perfect by six months. It does vary, though. Some puppies seem to get the idea pretty much straightaway while others are comparatively slow learners. Whichever category your pet belongs in—and most puppies fit somewhere in the middle—stick with the same routine patiently and make sure everyone else in the household does the same; the more consistent you are, the sooner your puppy will be clean.

HOW OFTEN DOES A PUPPY NEED TO GO?

There's no easy answer to this—it varies. It can include:

- When he wakes after a nap
- Straight after he eats
- When he's just had a lively game (or sometimes in the middle of a lively game!)
- When he's excited.

In the six-step guide on page 100, the suggestion is that you should take your puppy outside every hour, on the hour. He may not need to pee every time, but it's usually often enough to give you plenty of opportunities to praise and reinforce him when he does. Before long, you'll get used to your puppy's habits and be able to judge accurately when he's likely to need to go. At first, though, you should remember these four points and keep an eye on him for signs that he needs to go in between his hourly outings.

MAKING HIS WAY OUTDOORS

It can be tempting, when you spot your puppy circling and realize he's about to pee, to scoop him up in your arms and rush him out of doors. Ideally, though, it's better for him to learn as early as possible to get out of doors under his own steam. Instead of picking him up, try calling him in an excited, upbeat tone, then running to the door, encouraging him to follow you. Keep it fun and positive, as though you're involving him in a game—the ideal scenario is for him to run after you, perform out of doors in the right spot, and then be rewarded with a special treat: this is the perfect positive experience, which he'll want to repeat.

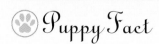

Puppy Fact

Your pup's instincts are on your side. Those animals that live in dens or nests in the wild prefer not to soil where they sleep. From the age of around three weeks most puppies will try to go to the bathroom away from their beds.

BEHIND THE SIGNS

You Give the Signs

When you're housebreaking, it can help if you try to see things from your puppy's point of view. He doesn't start with any "good" or "bad" connections with toileting indoors or out of doors—the way he learns which is the best place to go is from your reaction. So make sure that you sound thrilled with him when he manages to pick the right spot, and, equally, that your body language is neutral if you have to clear up an accident.

SIX STEPS TO HOUSETRAINING

1. Have some of your puppy's favorite treats on hand at all times, plus keep shoes and umbrella at the door so that you can rush out to the yard quickly with him whatever the weather.

2. Take your puppy outside at least once an hour and stay out with him. If he squats and eliminates, praise him warmly. If you're out there for more than a few minutes and he doesn't, come back inside with him.

3. In between times, keep an eye on him. Puppies give signs when they need to go—he might start to sniff around, stop what he's doing and look around him, or start to turn in circles. You're trying to catch him at the point before he actually squats. If you see any of these signs, call him cheerfully and speedily to the door and go out into the backyard with him.

4. If you didn't catch him in good time and you see him start to squat, make a sharp, sudden sound (it could be "uh-uh," "no-no," or similar—it needs to be sharp enough to catch your pup's attention, but not loud or fierce enough to be frightening). This will usually be enough to stop him for a moment. Then quickly encourage him outside.

5. Always praise when your puppy gets it right, and ignore accidents. As soon as he understands that going outside wins him praise and a treat, he'll try to do what you want. But accidents will happen; clean them up quietly, without confusing the lesson.

6. As your puppy begins to get the idea that he should go to the bathroom outdoors, add a verbal cue. Choose something short that you won't mind saying in front of other people—"Time to go!" or "Go now!" are two examples. Eventually, when your puppy's an adult dog, this is going to be his cue to perform on command. Wait until he's in the act of going and give him the cue before he finishes. As always, timing is important to build the association between the act and the consequence; the cue is given as he goes, and the praise and the treat the moment he's finished.

DEALING WITH ACCIDENTS

If you weren't quick enough and your puppy had an accident, don't scold him. There are several reasons why you should never punish a puppy for an accident indoors.

- He won't make the connection between the deed and the punishment—when an owner says, "he knew he shouldn't have done it; he looked guilty," all it means is that the puppy knew their owner was displeased and looked fearful of their reaction. Puppies don't experience "guilt" in the human sense.
- If you make him frightened of "going" in front of you, he may decide it's safer to take himself off to a corner where you can't see and go there. In the long run, this will slow down the housebreaking.
- It is always better when training to concentrate on what the pup should do, rather than on what he shouldn't. If you weren't quick enough to get him out of doors when he needed to go, that's your responsibility, not his.

HOW TO CLEAN UP

Your puppy's keen nose can smell where he went before, whether indoors or out, and this can act as a trigger to prompt him to go again. Outdoors, that's desirable (you can take him repeatedly to the same area in the yard and eventually he'll take it for granted that that's his toileting spot), but if he's had an accident indoors, you need to eliminate both the smell and the connection he makes with it. Just wiping the area down with disinfectant or a cleaner, particularly one with ammonia in it, won't get rid of the smell as far as your puppy is concerned, even if you think it's been thoroughly cleaned. Instead, clear up either with one of the products made for the purpose (you can buy these at any pet store), or with a solution of baking soda, or a dilute mix of biological laundry liquid. Any of these will work to discourage your puppy from picking the same spot again.

OVERNIGHT

Just like ours, puppies' systems slow down when they're asleep, and they need to go less often. Every puppy will have his own timetable; from the day that you bring him home, take him out last thing at night and be aware that he's likely to need to go again very early in the morning. If he's sleeping nearby (say, in a crate in your bedroom), then he'll probably whimper when he needs to go. If he does, get up and take him out as quickly as you can. If he's sleeping in an area away from you, like the kitchen, get up to take him out as early as you can. Be prepared for overnight accidents—very few young puppies will manage six or seven hours without needing to toilet. When he does start to get through the night without any mishaps, don't assume, just because he can hold on overnight, that he'll be able to last longer periods during the day, either—keep up the once-an-hour routine.

HOUSETRAINING MYTHS

There are a lot of myths that people may repeat while you're housetraining a new puppy. Most are just that, and you should ignore them. Here are five of the most common ones:

Myth: If he has an accident, simply rub his nose in it—he'll soon learn.
Fact: This would be counterproductive, as well as unkind—all your puppy would learn is that you can get angry for—in his mind—no reason, and as a result he will start to lose trust in you. He doesn't yet have the connection between praise and toileting out of doors, and that's what you're working to build.

Myth: He won't go if you keep him in an enclosed space.
Fact: There's a bit more truth in this one: puppies don't like to eliminate where they sleep (or eat), and that's why crate training can help with housetraining. A very young puppy has a limited amount of bladder control and will reach a point, often sooner than you might think, where he has to go wherever he happens to be at the time.

Myth: If you leave him outside by himself for a few minutes and then call him in, he'll go on his own.
Fact: He may go, or he may not. But if you're not with him to praise him when he does, you're not creating the link in his mind with going out of doors and good

things happening. Also, a sociable puppy left outdoors on his own is likely to be thinking about what you're up to back indoors—and is less likely to concentrate on the business in hand.

Myth: He'll learn to hold it more quickly if you leave it till the last minute between visits outdoors.
Fact: He won't—you'll simply have more accidents indoors. Sticking rigidly to the at-least-once-an-hour trips out of doors routine is the fastest way to reliable housetraining. If your pup has learned that your approval is the way to treats and praise, he will try to do what you want, but—see left—a small puppy's control over his bladder is very limited.

Myth: He's being slow to learn housetraining because he's a [insert breed of choice here]; they're well known to be hard to teach.
Fact: Your puppy is an individual, whether he's a dachshund, a German Shepherd or a mixed breed. How fast he learns his housetraining is part of his individual makeup; it's not breed-dependent. The only grain of truth here is that some research has shown that puppies from impoverished backgrounds (such as puppy farms) are slower to learn—both housetraining and training generally. It's another reason to make very sure of your puppy's early background.

TROUBLESHOOTING

Occasionally, you'll hit a glitch while housebreaking. If your puppy suddenly starts leaving puddles unpredictably, particularly if you previously felt that you were making progress with his housetraining, he may have an infection of the urinary tract. You should take him to the vet to be checked out—these infections in puppies aren't unusual and are easy to treat, but can affect your pet's overall health if ignored.

If your puppy regularly makes a puddle when greeting visitors or other dogs, chances are that this is a specific sign, in puppy talk. Technically it's called "submissive urination"; he's sending a message to the people or dog he's meeting that he's young and helpless and they should be gentle with him. The same puppy may send the same message by rolling over on his back, showing his belly, whenever he encounters anything or anyone he finds unfamiliar or intimidating. If your puppy does this, he may be generally a little timid in his approach to life, and you should pay extra care to his socialization, introducing him gradually and gently to new things and making sure not to overwhelm him with too many experiences at once. The puddles will usually stop happening as his confidence grows and he starts to look forward to visitors, human or canine, with happy anticipation, rather than apprehension.

The onset of sexual maturity can cause a hiccup in housetraining in both sexes, and your puppy may once again start to have the occasional accident in the house some time after you thought he was fully trained. If this happens, return to your original outside-every-hour housetraining routine. Your puppy should soon once again be clean indoors.

HOW YOU KNOW YOU'RE MAKING PROGRESS

When your puppy heads for the door of his own accord, or whines to get your attention because he needs to get outside, or when even an accident is on the paper nearest the door, you can feel confident that your puppy is getting the idea. Keep your own signals consistent, praising him when he manages to perform out of doors and clearing up any accidents indoors calmly and quietly.

No. 11 CRATES AND BASKETS

QUIET TIME FOR YOUR PUP

*Y*our puppy will need somewhere to go for quiet time — both for your sake and his own. Young puppies can easily become overwhelmed when dealing with all the changes in a new home, and need relatively frequent naps. Human opinions vary as to whether dogs prefer a basket or a crate, but either will work well if you get into a good routine early on.

CRATE OR BASKET?

Many dogs have both—a basket for sociable downtime and a crate for overnight sleeping. Crates don't have the visual appeal of a comfy blanket-lined basket, but they have definite advantages. A crate can be helpful as an aid to housetraining (see page 98) and, when your puppy is used to it and enjoys his rest time there, you can keep him in it for short periods if you need him to be safely out of the way. A puppy who has come to see his crate as his safe place can retreat there if he's finding everything too much—if he's being pestered by children when he's tired, for example.

Also, a dog who is used to being in a crate will easily accept one for car travel, which is especially useful if you sometimes need to make long journeys with your pet.

TOWELS AND BLANKETS

Crate or basket, with a young puppy in the house, you're going to need plenty of towels and blankets—puppies create extra laundry. Stock up with old, soft, washable bedding at thrift shops and garage sales. If your puppy came from a breeder and brought an old towel, a toy, or a comforter with him (many breeders will send something with every puppy to their new home), tuck it in with him at night; it will smell familiar and offer reassurance, helping him settle down.

If you opt for a crate, it's important to introduce the puppy to it carefully and to use it correctly.

CRATE DOS AND DON'TS

DO

- Set it up in a quiet corner where it can stay more or less permanently. Once your puppy gets used to his crate, it will become his refuge.

- Line it with a thick layer of newspaper on the floor, covered by washable towels or blankets, so that you can easily clean up if your puppy has an accident. A blanket over the top of the crate can also encourage your pup to see it as his "den."

- Always clean up promptly if a puppy soils his crate.

- Leave the door open all the time at first. It's important that your puppy starts to go to his crate of his own free will, and is happy spending time there. Encourage him to go to his crate by leaving treats in it.

- When your puppy is happily going into his crate on his own, practice shutting the door for a few seconds (ten is plenty), and then opening it again. You can gradually increase the time over two or three weeks, practicing every day.

As you increase the time, add extra treats that will engage him and take some time to finish to reinforce the idea that his crate is where good things happen.

DON'T

- Shut your puppy in his crate as a punishment. It's important that it should have only positive associations for him.

- Leave your puppy for prolonged periods in a shut crate, even after he is used to being there with the door closed. If he is sleeping there overnight, the door should be left open. If you want to confine him in a limited space overnight while he is still very young, leave the crate in a room where the door can be shut, but leave the crate door open.

- Confine a bigger puppy in a too-small crate. If you want to keep the same crate as your puppy grows, buy a crate divider that can be removed as he gets larger. Take your puppy with you to choose a crate and try different sizes out to ensure you pick the right one.

WHERE YOUR PUP SLEEPS

Decide where you'd like your puppy to sleep at night (he'll be taking frequent naps during the day at first, too, but you'll find puppies tend to fall asleep very suddenly—sometimes they'll keel over right in the middle of a game). Traditionally, the family dog had his own place in a warm corner of the kitchen, but you might opt for a spot on the landing, a corner of your bedroom or somewhere else—it doesn't matter where so long as it's neither on a main pathway through the house where there's constant activity and people passing through, nor in a spot too far away from all reassuring noise and activity; try to pick a happy medium. While your puppy isn't yet housetrained, you may opt for the laundry room or the kitchen if it has a hard floor, which makes cleaning up accidents much easier. Having chosen your spot, start to use a calming-down routine before bedtime at night.

It's natural to have a few disturbed nights directly after you bring your puppy home, while he gets used to being away from his mother and the other pups and acclimatizes to his new surroundings, but at the end of each busy day you'll have a tired puppy, and it should be fairly easy to settle him into a routine. Set up a series of steps that you go through every night, and he'll soon accept that it's bedtime.

Timing Is Crucial

If you're reassuring a whining pup, time any soothing you want to do very carefully—wait until you have a pause in the whimpering before reassuring him. Even if it's only a difference of a split second, puppies are supersensitive to your reactions, and if you get your timing right, you'll be reinforcing that he gets attention for being quiet, rather than playing up.

FIVE STEPS TO PUPPY BEDTIME

Young puppies may have as many as five meals a day; start the bedtime routine after your pup has had his final meal.

1. After your puppy has had the last meal of the day, take him out in the backyard for a pee break.

2. On your return to the house, set aside 15 minutes for an energetic romp with him—throw a ball, play with his toys, anything that uses up some evening energy.

3. Gradually wind down the energetic play and spend a further 15 minutes playing "learning" games—anything from "Sit" and "Leave" to rudimentary trick training. This sort of game makes your puppy think (and tires him), but without ramping up his energy levels.

4. Take your puppy on a final backyard visit. Stay out long enough to make sure he's done all he needs to do.

5. When you come in, go to his crate with him and place a few small treats or a chew toy in it. Allow him a minute or two to settle, then leave the room without any fuss, closing the door.

Some puppies get into the routine quickly; others will cry and make a fuss across a number of nights. If the puppy is in a corner of your room, you can make soothing noises, but try to keep it low-key, and if he wanders around, return him to his crate without making much fuss of him (if you use a puppy pen, you may want to put the crate into the pen for extra puppy security overnight). If he isn't in your room and you do feel you need to go in and check on him, spend a little time sitting in the room, but without paying him extra attention. Don't take him out of the room or spend extra time petting him, or you'll be teaching him

that fussing pays off. If he's lonely or scared, another presence in the room will reassure him, but if you're quiet and not paying him attention, you won't be reinforcing the crying.

DAYTIME NAPS

You may be able to let sleeping dogs lie, but leaving a sleeping puppy alone for any length of time is asking for trouble. During the day a young puppy will need frequent naps, but they probably won't be for long: often your pet will wake recharged—and ready to get into all kinds of mischief—just 15 or 20 minutes after he dropped off.

USING A PUPPY PEN

If you're busy it can be tempting to think "I'll just get this done" while your puppy is sleeping, but don't leave him unattended for more than a minute or two. If you really need to attend to something away from him for more than a few minutes, a purpose-made puppy pen or an old child's playpen can be useful to keep him safe for a short time. If you use a child's playpen, check that the bars are close enough together for him to be unable to escape (or get his head stuck between them if he wakes up and decides to mount a jailbreak); custom-built puppy pens are made of quite narrow wire grids that are clipped together and are easy and quick to put up and take down. Leave a few things to keep him occupied—a toy, a chew—while you leave him. Take him out for a pee break before you put him in the pen. He may opt to take a nap when he doesn't have the stimulation of company. And if you start him off sleeping in your own room, a pen may be useful to confine him to just a corner of it.

Activity Levels

Domestic dogs descend from predatory forebears: their wild ancestors hunted at dawn and at dusk, when the animals they preyed on came out to feed. Because of this, dogs still tend to be crepuscular—that is, hardwired to be most active at each end of the day: very early in the morning and in the evening. You may find that your puppy's energy levels follow this pattern, with a surge of extra activity just before bedtime.

YOUR PUPPY'S HEALTH

KEEPING YOUR PUPPY WELL

*W*hen you bring your puppy home, he'll usually be around eight weeks old, and will already have had his first vaccination. When you collect him, remember to ask for the papers that give the details for this—your vet will want to see them, and you need a complete health record for your puppy. Your priority as far as his health is concerned is to sign him up with a vet, so that he can complete his vaccination program, and have his check-ups as they fall due, and so that you have expert advice on call if any problems crop up.

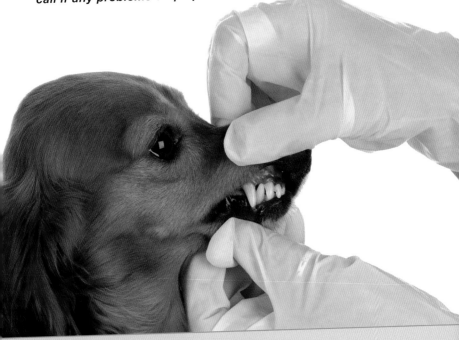

FINDING A VET

If you're not already with a veterinary practice, ask fellow dog owners for recommendations. Follow up with a call, to ask any questions you have and to chat through surgery practice with a vet before making an appointment. For example, you might want to know if there's 24-hour availability in an emergency, or, if you're keen on the possibility of holistic treatments for your pet, whether they are happy to arrange referrals. If you like the sound of the practice, ask if you can build in a "soft" first appointment to register your puppy: it can be part of his early socialization, and if he gets a great welcome at the desk and a few treats, you'll have laid the foundations for him to think of the vet's surgery as a good place to visit.

VACCINATION

Your puppy will always need at least one more shot in addition to the one he had before you brought him home. It is usually at 12 weeks, although some vets recommend it is given at ten; a third shot, at some point when your puppy is aged between four and six months, may also be recommended. The cover offered by vaccination may also vary somewhat according to where you live—it always protects against a number of common diseases, but it's possible to get vaccinations that guard against a broader range of problems. Core diseases that are always covered, regardless of where you live, are parvovirus, distemper, and hepatitis. Other vaccines may be recommended according to local conditions—for example, leptospirosis is usually included as standard in puppy vaccinations in the UK, and similarly, vaccination against rabies is standard in North America. Vaccination does carry a small risk of allergic or other negative reactions, though, and many experts advise against overloading a puppy's immune system. (In addition, in research tests, a few breeds, including, for example, Weimaraner and Dachshund, have been shown to have a slightly stronger chance of a negative reaction to immunization than others; your vet may specify a lighter immunization schedule in these cases.) Ask your vet to clarify exactly what diseases are covered in your puppy's vaccinations. Immunity is sustained by booster injections, the first always given a year after your puppy's second vaccination. Boosters may subsequently be given either annually or every three years; again, check with your vet what his practice is regarding this. Whichever booster schedule is recommended, make sure that you remember to take your pup for his shots promptly; the diseases the booster protects against can be extremely serious, so it's important that his immunity is maintained.

Be aware that, although it's extremely unusual, it is possible for your puppy to contract one of the diseases that his immunization should guard against in the period between losing the natural immunity he got from his mother and his final immunization shot from the vet. For this reason, you should always keep an eye on him and call the vet sooner rather than later if he seems lethargic or has any worrying symptoms, such as repeated vomiting, that last more than a few hours.

INSURANCE

To insure or not to insure? Some owners feel that vet fees for a young dog are unlikely to come to more than the (often fairly high) insurance premiums, while others take the "better safe than sorry" approach. Whichever camp you fall into, go through the options carefully if you're considering insurance for your pup, as cover varies widely and you'll want to pick the right policy. Feel free to discuss the pros and cons with the insurer over the phone before committing to insurance.

Questions to ask:
- Will the premium be reviewed annually? (Many premiums go up whether or not you have made a claim.)
- Exactly what does the policy cover? Ideally, your puppy's insurance should cover treatment needed for infections or diseases, treatment needed as a result of accidents, and treatment needed

for any previously unidentified health problems. Many insurers make breed-specific exclusions (for example, the insurance may not cover treatment for hip problems in breeds known to suffer widely from hip dysplasia, common in, for example German Shepherds), and you need to be clear about these. Usually, as with other types of insurance, there will be an excess figure at which the insurance kicks in—that is, you will pay for any treatment up to a certain amount, and if the treatment costs more than this amount, the insurance will cover it. Excess figures vary quite widely, so check that you're happy with the excess on your specific policy.
- Provided that your puppy has been immunized, in the unlikely event that he contracts one of the conditions that immunization guards against, will the policy cover his treatment?

PARASITES AND YOUR PUPPY

The range of parasites from which dogs can suffer is broad, but a healthy puppy

Puppy Fact

Colostrum, the milk that the mother feeds her puppies in their first few days of life, contains antibodies that give them some protection against infection. This is known as "passive" immunity and it gradually fades through the first four months of life; by the age of 12–14 weeks, most puppies will no longer have any degree of natural immunity.

is unlikely to suffer from very many of them. The two exceptions, which the majority of puppies will have at some point in their first six months—one internal, the other external—are worms and fleas. Treatment is twofold: first you need to get rid of any parasites he has, then make sure he has the right products to prevent their return.

Worms

Various kinds of worms, in particular roundworms, are extremely common in puppies—many are actually born with them. They're harmful because they take nutrients away from the growing puppy and can compromise his health by causing an overall loss in stamina and condition. Puppies who eat ravenously but remain rather thin may be suffering from a heavy infestation. A responsible breeder will have first wormed your puppy when he was two weeks old, then again at four to five weeks, and a third time at eight weeks, just before he came to you, and will give you the dates at which he was wormed, along with his immunization dates, with his paperwork when you come to take him home. If the breeder doesn't volunteer this information, do ask—it's an important aspect of your pup's health.

Your vet should prescribe a wormer at your puppy's first surgery visit—depending on the medicine, you may be advised to worm your puppy either monthly or quarterly. Do use the recommended treatment—cheaper, non-prescription wormers that you can buy at the pet store may not be appropriate for your puppy and aren't always effective.

Hot Spots

In some puppies, flea bites can result in an extreme skin inflammation called "hot spots." These are the result of an allergy to flea saliva—they are red areas of skin that are hot and damp to the touch and the irritation is so intense that the puppy can't stop scratching, which can result in infection. If your puppy has these symptoms, take him to the vet straightaway: he will probably need specific medicine for the problem, and flea treatment and prevention on their own will not be enough to clear it up.

Fleas

If your puppy scratches a lot, or shows signs of skin irritation, the most likely culprits are fleas. They don't live on him; they jump on to him when they're hungry and feed on his blood, then jump off again when they've fed, so if he has fleas, you have to flea-treat both the puppy and your home. It's not hard to get rid of fleas, but you have to be both consistent and persistent to eliminate them completely.

First, treat your puppy. For a young puppy, the vet may suggest a flea collar that has been treated with a flea repellent. If he is slightly older, he may be prescribed a tablet to be taken internally, or one of a number of skin treatments that are applied topically. These generally come in the form of a tiny tube of liquid that is placed directly on the skin, usually on the back of your puppy's neck. If you're using a topical treatment, be sure to part the fur so that the liquid makes contact with the skin, and, if necessary, ask someone

to help you while you apply it—it can be tricky to get the liquid in the right place while you're also trying to hold a squirming puppy. Your vet will usually stipulate that your puppy shouldn't be bathed for 48 hours after having the treatment applied. Next, de-flea your house. You can buy numerous products in the form of special shampoos, washes, and sprays to make the job easier—wash all your puppy's bedding and either wash or spray soft furnishings and carpets. Be prepared to repeat the cycle a couple of times before your puppy and your house are completely free of fleas. Once you've managed it, keeping them that way is relatively easy: you simply have to be conscientious about regularly treating your pet with the prescribed anti-flea product.

Other parasites

Mites and ticks are the other parasites that are commonly a nuisance with puppies. When your puppy has

completed his immunization and is out and about, and particularly if he is walked in rural or wooded areas, he may attract a few ticks. Like fleas, ticks are blood-suckers; members of the same family as spiders, they attach themselves to the puppy's skin with hooked mouthparts.

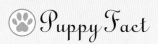

Puppy Fact

If you suspect he has fleas but you're not sure, take a fine-toothed comb and a piece of tissue and comb the area just above his tail carefully. If black specks fall onto the tissue, dampen it, and if they then turn reddish, your puppy has fleas. The specks are flea feces.

General Health

Just like small children, puppies can become ill quite quickly— and can recover just as fast. If you're not sure if your puppy is ill, always err on the side of caution and take them to the vet for a check-up within 24 hours. In particular, call the vet if he has either excessive vomiting or diarrhea: puppies can get dehydrated in a short time, so he needs medical attention fast.

They are usually a greyish color and can range in size from a pinhead to almost the size of a pea if they've been feeding on your puppy for a while (and they're another reason why you should check your puppy all over a couple of times a week). They can cause a wide range of infections and, ideally, prevention is better than cure; as well as examining your puppy carefully when you're grooming him, use a tick-repellent product if he's regularly walked anywhere where there's thick undergrowth. If you do find a tick on your pup, use tweezers to pull it away, gently but firmly, and dab the bite area with an antibiotic ointment to deter infection.

If your puppy constantly shakes his head from side to side, or scratches at his ears with his paw, the most likely culprits are ear mites. They can't always be seen, although inside your puppy's ears may look grubby and produce more and darker wax than usual if he has mites. If you suspect he has them, take him to your veterinarian, who will prescribe drops to get rid of them.

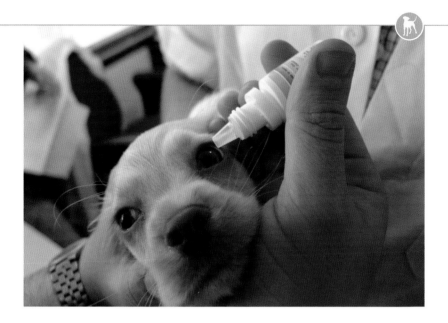

GIVING MEDICINE

At some point you'll have to give pills or ear- or eye-drops to your puppy. Here's how to do it easily.

Pills

Pills are best disguised in food—push a pill into a small piece of cheese, or wrap it in ham or a little chicken. If you have to give a puppy a large pill, break it into pieces before disguising. Watch your puppy until you're sure he's swallowed it; some pups are good at eating the food and neatly discarding the pill.

Ear drops

Hold the flap of the ear open and drip the drops deep into the ear. Continue to hold your puppy for a few seconds and gently massage the outer base of the ear to help the drops go down; if you release him immediately, a vigorous shake of his head can send the drops flying out of the ear before they have the chance to do any good.

Eye drops

Some puppies are prone to conjunctivitis and other eye infections. If your vet prescribes eye drops, get the dropper ready before you pick up the puppy, then gently hold his head still and drip the medicine into his eye. (You may need someone to help by holding him so that you can aim the drops accurately.) Continue to hold him until he has blinked a few times after the drops have gone in; this ensures that they are distributed across the eye's surface and he can't shake them out again.

BODY LANGUAGE

LEARNING TO READ YOUR PUPPY

*W*hen you first bring a puppy home it can feel as though, except when he's asleep, he's in constant motion. How can you learn to read such a small animal when he seems to cartwheel through every day? As you gradually get to know him and become familiar with his personality, you'll begin to see the signs that tell you how he's feeling: whether he's happy, fearful, feisty, sleepy....

Dogs can't speak. But their body language is extremely expressive, if you learn to read it. This section will give you a good start in understanding what your puppy is saying— both to people and to other dogs. It takes a quick trip around your dog and shows you how to interpret all the signs that he's constantly sending you with his body, from ears to tail. After that, you can learn more simply by observing how different dogs mix, both with other dogs and with people.

HAPPY AND CONFIDENT

When your puppy is feeling happy and outgoing, his tail will be up but held relaxed (not stiffly), his mouth will be loose, without any tension in his muzzle, and his eyes will be naturally open, neither narrowed nor wide and rounded. If he's trying to entice another dog into play, he may go into the classic "play bow," with front end down low, forepaws extended, and his tail and hindquarters in the air. His ears may be slightly forwards if he's concentrating on something interesting. A happy puppy may have exaggeratedly bouncy movements, too, particularly when he's playing.

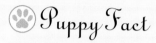

Puppy Fact

Just as an adult human will talk in a more sophisticated way than a young child would, so studies have shown that puppies gradually refine the way they use their bodies to express themselves as they mature, and their body language gains fluency and confidence. While the basic body language toolkit seems to be both instinctive and universal, the way in which puppies use it is learned as they observe its effect on those around them.

INTERESTED BUT CAUTIOUS

A pup's body language may change when he meets the unfamiliar—an adult dog who is new to him, for example. Some puppies will confidently climb all over an adult (and may get a canine slapdown in response), but others approach with caution. They may use a range of so-called "calming signals" to slow down a direct encounter. These signals, a very clear sign language, were first noticed and identified by the eminent Norwegian trainer and author Turid Rugaas in a study in the 1980s, and they're often some of the earliest instinctive body language you see a puppy use. They might include looking away from the older dog, sitting down and scratching, yawning, and sniffing the ground, and are intended to convey that the puppy's intentions are friendly and not confrontational. In human terms, the puppy is simply being polite. If the older dog approaches the puppy and sniffs it, the puppy may behave even more deferentially, rolling over onto his back or submissively licking the older dog's muzzle. Your pup may use the same body language when meeting new people, too. A yawn, a quick flick of the tongue over his nose, or a glance away from the new person are all signs of caution, or, if used over and over again, even apprehension. The message that they send you is that your pup should be allowed to approach the newcomer at his own speed, rather than being pressed into an up-close introduction before he's ready.

FEARFUL

A puppy who has moved beyond mere caution into fear is easy to spot. His eyes will be wide and rounded, possibly with a little of the white showing; his back will be rounded and his posture stiff and still. His tail will be lowered and perhaps tucked between his back legs and his ears may be flattened to his head, too. Any or all of this body language is telling you that your pet needs support. If it's happening in response to the presence of another dog or a person, allow him to get further away from the source of his stress, to a point at which he's more comfortable. Don't do too much petting and soothing, though—this tends to reinforce his impression that there was something to be frightened about in the first place. Support him by keeping your own body language relaxed and confident. If he makes moves to run and hide, let him go.

When your puppy is showing signs of real fear, always take him seriously, and never force him into direct contact with whatever it is that he's afraid of. Fear is believed to be the number one factor behind behavioral problems in older dogs, so it needs to be taken seriously. The best way to deal with it is to expose your pup to the things he's afraid of, but only in extremely short and managed amounts, and to do your best to build a positive association rather than a negative one. The classic example is to have a stranger throw treats from some distance away for a puppy who's afraid of unfamiliar people, without attempting any direct contact, even when the puppy moves nearer, until the puppy himself initiates it.

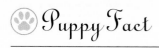

Puppy Fact

In dog language, a direct stare signifies a threat: dogs don't usually look each other in the eye, instead using indirect glances. When your puppy looks away or deflects his gaze from yours, he's showing respect toward you.

Puppy Appeasement

Puppies come hard-wired to deflect any frightening response from an adult dog. Rolling on his back tells you that he's no threat, as does producing a small amount of urine. When a puppy tries to get up to your face to lick it, he's copying the way he licked his mother's face when he was very young. In wolves and wild dogs this licking prompts the mother dog to regurgitate food for her young to eat—domestic dogs no longer do this, but the puppy's instinct remains. These so-called appeasement gestures are the baby version of the calming signals that fluent adult dogs will use as a useful part of their body-language repertoire.

WHAT ABOUT AGGRESSIVE OR DOMINANT BODY LANGUAGE?

It's rare to see reactions that could be defined as aggressive in a puppy—while he's small, fearful reactions and appeasement gestures are likely to protect him best. But a very confident, outgoing puppy may react with something that looks to us like anger when he's frustrated. A puckered muzzle, with the lips pulled back from the teeth, a stiff, still stance, and an upright tail that wags slowly, very unlike the loose wag of a happy puppy, are all signs to take note of. "Dominance" is an expression much less used by animal behaviorists today than it was in the past, as it has led to all kinds of myths about the need for human owners to "dominate" their dogs in order to assert themselves over their pets. If your puppy's body language tells you that he reacts badly to being frustrated, he may need longer and more patient training than a more placid-natured dog would. You must ensure that the bond you build with him is strong enough to override his urge to sort difficult situations out for himself.

THEY DO *WHAT?*

Unless they're very elderly or very grumpy, most adult dogs seem to have a built-in tolerance of puppy rudeness, and will put up with being clambered over, having their ears swung on, and numerous other affronts from very young puppies with only the occasional protest.

When a puppy reaches a certain age, though, usually at about between five and six months, a natural cut-off point occurs and all but the most relaxed dogs will begin to teach the adolescent dog canine manners. Disapproval of pushy behavior on the puppy's part may be shown quite subtly at first—with a wrinkling of the muzzle, or a low growl, almost too quiet for human ears to hear. If the puppy persists in being boorish, this may escalate, with the older dog putting on a fierce display—air snapping, or escalating the growl to a level at which the puppy draws back. Although it can be alarming, and noisy, to watch there's rarely any need for human intervention: most of these displays are just that, and don't usually end in any kind of aggressive contact. In human terms, they're the equivalent of a grown-up, having tolerated a pushy child, insisting on better manners when that child turns into a rude teenager.

WATCHING PUPPIES PLAY

When your puppy meets a canine friend, or if he attends puppy classes or parties, take the opportunity to stand back and simply watch them play. It's an appealing activity in its own right, but if you watch a pair of puppies, or better still a larger group, for 15 or 20 minutes, you will be surprised by just how many tiny, different sorts of "language" exchange you spot. It's a good exercise to read the different ways in which they express their intentions and go for the different things they want: gaining possession of a toy, enticing another puppy into play, or asking for downtime are all easy to see as they interact with one another.

And watching over a period reveals a lot of subtleties about individual character, too—you may notice, for instance, how a puppy that seems to be easygoing or even submissive is nevertheless often the one that gets possession of the most coveted toy by persisting with body language that may look subservient (with sustained groveling and face-licking, perhaps) but which will ultimately exasperate the apparently more confident puppy into giving it up. Try to make it a habit to take a few minutes to observe your puppy mixing with dogs, humans or a mixture of both every day: it will teach you more about the way he engages with the world than a book ever could.

PUPPY CONFUSION

Few well-socialized puppies have problems understanding what other dogs are telling them. Human body language isn't nearly as clear to them. Look out for signs that your puppy is telling you that he's confused or worried about what you expect of him. Owners sometimes interpret these signs as indications that their puppy is ignoring them and not paying attention to what he is being asked to do. Far from it, the puppy is usually trying to send a message, as he would to another dog, that he's not sure what's expected and he doesn't want you to get impatient with him. Look out for a puppy sitting down at an angle to you (non-confrontational), suddenly scratching, or keenly sniffing around when he doesn't need to go out. And yawning and quick flicks of the tongue over the nose are signs, too. If your puppy performs any or all of these repeatedly when you're trying to teach him something, back up and slow down the exercise until his body language relaxes and tells you he's comfortable again.

GETTING EVERYONE INVOLVED

*U*nless you live on your own (in which case, this chapter still holds for visiting family and friends), it's good to have everyone in the household involved in raising your puppy.

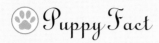

Puppy Fact

If your puppy were a person, he'd be fitting ten years' worth of growth and learning into his first six months. Remember this when he seems slow to pick something up: he's actually learning at a phenomenal rate.

This doesn't mean that he shouldn't have a primary carer—and since you're reading this book, this should probably be you: the central person who is responsible for seeing that he's fed and exercised, who checks that his socialization is being attended to, and sees that, generally, he's well looked after and happy. But the more people who are around him every day, with whom he interacts, and from whom he gets consistent signals about his behavior, the more likely he is to grow up happy and confident in all kinds of surroundings. And training your family is the quickest route to training your dog!

KEEPING THINGS SIMPLE

Your puppy will learn to fit in more quickly if he knows what to expect. There are two parts to this: first, that everyone around him behaves consistently with him; and

second, that he has a routine that, by and large, is followed every day. A puppy's life is always full of novelty and excitement; he'll see to that himself, as he discovers the world around him. But the basic underpinnings, from meals to bedtime, should stay the same.

CONSISTENCY

From the day he arrives, have some rules for behavior around the puppy. Write them down, have a family meeting to make sure everyone knows about them, and then stick them on the refrigerator door as a reminder. Examples might be:

- Do remember to praise the puppy when he does what you want.
- Do take the puppy outside right away if he's circling, sniffing the ground, or showing other signs that he needs to go. (Housetraining is going to be easier if everyone in the household is aware of what these signs are, and what to do if they see them.)
- Do handle the puppy gently—remember, even quite young children are going to look huge to him, so try not to intimidate him.
- Don't feed the puppy from the table, or if you are snacking elsewhere.
- Don't rev up the puppy's energy after his final playtime, when you should be trying to calm him down before bed.
- Don't play rough with the puppy; handle him gently.

SETTING UP A SCHEDULE

A typical day's schedule for an eight-week puppy who is being fed four meals a day and who is in the process of housetraining might go something like this. It may look a bit daunting at first to have every half hour accounted for, but if the whole household knows about it, then it's easy to delegate parts of it to different family members. It gets the puppy used to what to expect next, and reconciles him to having quiet times when he needs to settle down. You can tailor it to work around you (for example, you could combine the school run with a socialization exercise for your pup).

7:00am	Wake up. Outside for toileting
7:30am	Breakfast
8:00am	Outside for toileting
8:30am	Playtime
9:00am	Outside for toileting
9:30am	Quiet time in the crate or puppy-pen
10:00am	Outside for toileting
10:30am	Short training session
11:00am	Outside for toileting
11:30am	Socialization exercise (e.g. a short grooming session, meeting someone new, being introduced to another dog, a short car trip)
12 noon	Second meal
12:30pm	Outside for toileting
1:00pm	Playtime
1:30pm	Outside for toileting
2:00pm	Quiet time
2:30pm	Outside for toileting
3:00pm	Socialization exercise
3:30pm	Third meal
4:00pm	Outside for toileting
4:30pm	Playtime
5:00pm	Outside for toileting
5:30pm	Quiet time
6:00pm	Outside for toileting
6:30pm	Fourth meal
7:00pm	Outside for toileting
7:30pm	Evening social time— the opportunity to be with the family as a group, perhaps in the living room. Playtime, followed by a short group training session.
8:00pm	Outside for toileting—last visit outside
8:30pm	Bedtime

GETTING INTO A ROUTINE

As your puppy's housetraining settles, he's fed fewer, larger meals, and—after his immunization is complete—he's able to go for walks. His routine will become less demanding and downtime periods, when he settles down both in your company and, gradually, on his own, will get longer. In the meantime, over the first two or three busy months, getting the household working as a team will help see that he's properly looked after while allowing everyone to manage their own routines.

WHEN YOU'RE BUSY

Rather than keeping a huge range of toys scattered around so that the puppy can pick up whatever he wants whenever he wants, create a toy bag or box. His toys can be tidied into this after playtime, and it can contain a range of other things from small hide chews to empty cardboard tubes or boxes, or even a sheet or two of newspaper crumpled into a ball—anything that he can safely play with, either by himself or with someone else joining in. Hang the bag from a hook somewhere obvious, like the back of the kitchen door, so that everyone knows where it is and can reach into it when the moment arises. Puppies will keep themselves entertained if they have something enticing to play with, and this needn't be a purpose-made toy—even a cardboard tube can provide a few minutes' fun. Having toys available on

rotation, so they're not all out all the time, will help to maintain your puppy's interest in them. A toy bag can also be useful when the puppy's found something he shouldn't be playing with—you can grab something from it, offer it in exchange, and turn the "He's got hold of the remote!" panic into an impromptu game.

CHILDREN AND YOUR PUPPY

Everyone remembers the much-loved family dog from their childhood. Children and puppies, with their similar energy levels and constant exploration of their surroundings, have a lot in common. Children have to be trained to treat puppies appropriately. Having their own dog is a good opportunity to teach children how to behave around dogs in general, which can avoid situations where they may be bitten by behaving unwisely with a dog they don't know. Children over ten can simply be told; younger children, particularly toddlers, should always be watched when interacting with the puppy.

How your puppy feels about children will partly depend on his personality—a pup who is by nature outgoing and rather fearless may prove more bombproof than a timid puppy who tends to retreat rather than advance. But even timid dogs can learn to get along well with "their" children if the relationship is carefully managed by an adult.

Teach small children how to handle the puppy gently—this can be part of the puppy's socialization exercises, too. Most dogs like to be stroked under the chin or along their sides. They don't like being patted on top of the head, or anywhere where they can't see what an approaching hand is doing, and almost all dogs, even puppies, aren't keen on having their paws handled. Involve children in your puppy's grooming routine so that you can show them what he likes and what he doesn't. Keep a particularly sharp eye on children

who are at the crawling, or just walking stage: they present a challenge to a puppy. In particular, dogs don't like being stared at; direct eye contact between dogs is used as a threat, so if a small child "eyeballs" a puppy, the puppy may feel that he needs to defend himself.

NOISE AND ENERGY LEVELS

Puppies find high-pitched noises and sudden movements very exciting. If children are playing noisily, the puppy will join in and, if he gets overstimulated, may nip, catching clothing or, even more unluckily, skin. Most puppy bites happen either when a puppy is frightened and backed into a corner, or when he's been allowed to become hysterically overexcited. If your puppy and children are playing together, monitor them quite closely; if things are getting too rowdy, move in, call time out, and suggest an alternative activity to calm everyone down.

QUIET TIME

Build the bond between your puppy and your children by encouraging them to enjoy quiet time together. For example, if you read a bedtime story before your child goes to sleep, have the puppy alongside you or in your lap as you read. The child can gently pet the puppy and at the end of the day they'll both be sleepy and relaxed, creating a peaceful, pleasant experience for both.

TEASING

Don't ever allow children to tease your puppy. Holding out toys or food, then snatching them away or rolling the puppy over and holding him down when he's trying to get away can make him afraid of human contact in general. Small children don't always understand when they're being unkind, so explain why some things aren't a good idea. If the puppy is resting in his crate or basket, don't allow them to disturb him, either: he needs to know that he can go there as a refuge when he needs to.

BEHIND THE SIGNS

Avoid Guarding

You should have a general family rule that no one is allowed to bother your puppy while he's eating. However, there's one way you can avoid resource guarding (something that can be a particular problem around children) that usually works. While your puppy is still very small (and it hasn't yet occurred to him to "guard" his food), move the bowl slightly toward you while he's eating and add a little more food. Make sure he sees you do this. If he learns that having his bowl moved means that he gets more food, he's more likely to grow up to be relaxed around his dinner.

TRAINING YOUR PUPPY

WHAT TO AIM FOR

*W*hen you're training your pup, you want the end result to be a dog who's mastered the basics: sits and stays on request, walks nicely by your side when he's on a leash and, when off leash, comes back to you when called. These are all achievable, although to have a pet who manages every one 100 percent of the time will take plenty of practice. You can start training as soon as you bring your puppy home.

KEEP IT FUN

Ideally, your puppy shouldn't know he's being "trained." He should simply think that he's having fun with you and getting lots of attention along with his favorite treats. Aim for at least three sessions every day of no more than two to three minutes each—for a young puppy, that's plenty. If you're both enjoying yourselves, you can gradually increase the time to sessions of five minutes each, which should be the maximum for a puppy aged under six months—it's better to quit while he's still engaged and enjoying himself than waiting until he's tiring and beginning to lose concentration. As with all exercises with your pet, keep your tone light and upbeat and concentrate on your timing—it needs to be split-second

accurate to be successful. Even if he's slow to get the point of an exercise, never raise your voice or shout, or show other signs of impatience—he'll pick up on your exasperation and find it harder to concentrate. Try ending each session with a minute or two of play—encouraging him to chase you or playing with a toy together; it's another way of reinforcing his impression that this is all fun. When you've made good progress with the core things that you really need him to master, you could add a few tricks if you want— it's always nice having something the two of you can show off to visitors—and your puppy won't see any difference between learning "Sit" and learning to "Shake hands," provided you keep the praise and treats coming.

BEHIND THE SIGNS

What He's Saying

A recent study asked a number of professional trainers to observe owners practicing training exercises with their puppies. The results showed that, nine times out of ten, the puppy was responding to its owner's body language rather than their verbal cues. The message? Be aware of what your body is telling your puppy, as well as what your voice is saying. And give him space to get it right—don't crowd him or block him while he's trying to figure out what it is that you want him to do.

GET IT RIGHT, THEN ADD A VERBAL CUE

When you're teaching your puppy, even a simple "Sit" is a three-part process. First, the puppy needs to understand what it is that you want him to do, then he needs to do it, and finally he needs to do it on receiving a prompt from you. Generally, it's best to teach the action, then add the cue that tells him that it's that specific action you want from him. If you add the cue before he's completely clear on the action it represents he's likely to get confused.

WHERE TO TRAIN

When you're starting out, train your puppy in a quiet place where there aren't any distractions. Apart from "Watch me!" (which is the very first thing you'll teach him), indoors is best, so he won't have his attention diverted by traffic noise or tweeting birds. Ideally, you should start off training him in a room that has enough clear space for you both to move around freely. As you start to get results, you can gradually test his concentration by moving to an area with more distractions—perhaps in the living room with other people around, or out in the backyard, and eventually, when he's really getting the hang of it, in the park or recreation ground with lots of other things going on around you. Let him set the pace as he's learning (never add a new element before he's mastered the

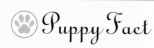

Puppies perform best when they know the rewards are substantial. Keep something small, smelly, and delicious reserved for training sessions only—tiny pea-sized pieces of liver, chicken, or cheese are all likely to be popular, but try various foods to find what your puppy likes best, and to guarantee an enthusiastic training partner. When you start out, you'll be feeding a lot of treats, so cut down very slightly on your puppy's meals to balance things out if you

last one). Practice one-offs outside your short training sessions, too—ask him for a "sit" at random times during the day, so that he understands that this is all-round behavior that can be requested at any time. And be ready to treat him when he obliges.

SHOULD HE WEAR A LEASH?

Your puppy shouldn't need to be on a leash for the first exercises. You won't be teaching him by forcing or pulling him—he'll be getting into position of his own accord. If you're working outdoors, at the local park for example, once you're reinforcing his training, he should be wearing a leash even if you're not holding the other end of it, just so you can pick it up if something happens and you need to have him under control.

TEACHING "WATCH ME!"

This is the very first cue your puppy needs to learn. Before you can teach him anything at all, his attention needs to be focused on you. Unusually you can start this exercise in the backyard if you like—you don't have to be indoors. Ideally you should be somewhere where there are things that will catch your puppy's attention for a moment or two, but nothing so distracting that it will hold his attention exclusively. Then you have to wait until he glances towards you. Don't call him or send any other signals, and don't lure him with a treat. Just sit or stand quietly until he looks at you. This exercise calls for precision timing: at the exact instant that he looks at you, praise him warmly and give him the treat. Stay still, wait until he looks at you again, then praise and treat him, again doing your best to catch the moment that his attention turns on you. Repeat a few

Split-second Timing

In a puppy's mind, a treat comes when he's doing the right thing, so be careful when you give it—he must receive it at the exact moment he's in the process of doing what you want him to do. So for a "Sit," he needs to be in the action of sitting as he gets the treat, and for a "Stay" he needs actually to be staying, not in the process of getting up from a stay. Careful observation and quick reactions on your part will help you get it right.

times until he's paying attention to you and only you, and he's had a few treats, then finish the session. Repeat two or three times a day, whenever you have a few spare minutes. When he's got to the stage of constantly glancing at you, thinking that a treat might be forthcoming, add the cue, saying "Watch me!" as he looks over at you. Soon, even a very quiet "Watch me!" will be enough to get his attention instantly.

TEACHING "SIT"

As soon as you know that you can get your puppy to concentrate on you, you can start teaching him to sit on command.

1. First he needs to understand what you want. Stand face-to-face with him, but a little way away, so you're not towering over him. Hold a treat in your hand and bring it down near enough to his nose for him to smell it (but not so close that he can make a grab for it).

2. Once you have his attention, move the treat up and over the back of his head. Keep your hand close to his head, not too high above it. As he raises his nose to follow the smell, his bottom will automatically go down, and he should go into a natural sit.

3. The moment his bottom touches the floor, give him the treat and tell him what a good dog he is. He'll probably get up to acknowledge the praise—and you can repeat the exercise. Two or three times per session is plenty.

What if he backs away from your hand as you move it, rather than sitting down?

Pick a place to practice where he's in a corner or near a wall and he can't back away; that way, the sit should come automatically.

4. When he's sitting promptly as you start to move your hand over his head, add the verbal cue—"Sit!" Time it at the exact moment that your hand moves; that way, as he gets more familiar with the exercise, he'll start to anticipate what you want with a sit before you lure him with the treat. Eventually, with plenty of practice, he'll sit as soon as you say the word.

Spend plenty of short session time on "Sit"; as well as being the simplest, it's also one of the most useful commands, and both "Down" and "Stay" start with a reliable "Sit" from your pup.

TEACHING "DOWN"

It's useful if your puppy will lie down on request (eventually this can be a part of asking him to settle down and be calm). The technique for teaching him "Down" is the same as for sit—first you lure him into the right position and then you gradually build a connection between the position and the command. And because the steps for "Down" actually need to begin with the puppy in a sit, it makes sense to teach the two together.

1. Start with your puppy sitting down (you can combine the "Sit" and "Down" requests in a sequence if you like).

2. Hold a treat near your puppy's nose so that he can smell it. Take your hand down from his nose to the floor, slowly, so you're luring him to follow it.

1. Start with your puppy in a sit. Stand in front of him.

2. Raising your hand upright, palm near his face, step backwards a couple of paces. Keep your hand steady, palm facing him—this is the visual clue he's to learn.

3. It may take several tries; if he doesn't move down, but instead "mugs" your hand for the treat, simply pull your hand back, wait until he sits, then bring the treat back near his nose and repeat the process. Eventually he'll lie down. The minute he manages it, give him the treat—before he gets up again!

4. Add the verbal cue exactly as you did with "Sit"—when he understands what you want and is reliably lying down as you take the treat to the floor, start to say "Down" and treating him at the moment he's moving to a lie-down. Timing, as always, is key.

TEACHING "STAY!"

At first, expect only very short "Stays" from your puppy—even a second or two deserves a treat, as this is one of the commands that most dogs find slightly harder to learn. Rather than asking him to do something (sit, or lie down) you're asking him not to do something (begin to move as you move away from him), and that's a more abstract idea for him to grasp.

3. Reward the shortest stay, even if it's only a second. While he is still in the stay, praise him and give him a treat. You may need fast reactions—because you want to reward him while he's still sitting, not at the moment he's getting up.

4. If he doesn't make any attempt to stay but gets up and moves as you move, go back to your original positions, ask him to sit, and try again. Don't treat him, but don't make a drama out of it either. He'll get it eventually.

5. In your first sessions on "Stay," aim to get him to stay consistently, rather than getting him to stay for a longer time. When you know he's going to stay when you ask, you can start to ask him to stay for more than just a few seconds.

6. When he's managing short stays consistently, add the verbal cue—say "Stay" as you make the palm-out sign with your hand.

When he's staying on the verbal command every time you ask, try increasing the distance between you by a few steps. But take it slowly and be absolutely consistent with the timing of the cue and of the reward.

TEACHING "COME!"

Reliable recall is absolutely invaluable in an adult dog. You want your pet to come when he's called, even if he's having a good time with plenty of distractions at the other side of the park. And the way to get that result is to start early and to have fairly modest expectations along the way. At first you're going to teach your puppy to come to you across a short distance when there's nothing else going on. You can either start this exercise when your puppy has learned a fairly reliable "Stay," or you can enlist a friend or family member to hold the puppy when you're moving away from him.

1. Start with the puppy either in a "Stay" or being held by someone else. At first, you're likely to need a helper for this exercise.

2. Holding a treat in your hand, move back a few paces (further than you usually would for a stay—perhaps the length of the room).

3. Bend or crouch slightly, hold out your arms, and call "Come!" in a warm,

upbeat voice. As you do, your helper should let the puppy go.

4. Your puppy will probably rush over to you. Greet him as exuberantly as you like—feel free to go slightly over the top. He should feel that coming to you is good fun. The more positive associations you can build with this exercise, the more likely he is to develop a solid recall as he gets older.

5. As you greet him, gently touch his collar and hold him while you give him the treat. It's important that you give him the treat while you are holding his collar. Keep your touch as light as you can; don't grab at him or pull at his collar. As soon as he's had the treat, release him.

There's a reason for this final step: many adult dogs will rush up to their owner when they're called, but then dance around him, refusing to be put on a leash and turning their owner's efforts to catch them into a game. By praising your pup when he comes to you, but retaining the treat until you're actually holding him, you're laying the foundations of a recall where your dog not only comes to you, but waits to have his leash put on when he arrives.

WHAT SHOULD YOU DO IF HE DOESN'T RUSH OVER?

Attracted by the treat and the fuss, 99 percent of puppies will head straight for you. If yours is in the one percent minority, work on him both during the exercise and when you're outside, playing, in a larger space. No puppy can resist a game of chase—so call him, then turn and run away from him. When he catches up with you, make a fuss of him in exactly the same way that you do during the "Come!" exercise. He'll soon grasp the idea.

TEACHING ON-LEASH WALKING

No one enjoys walking a dog who's perpetually pulling on the leash, so your puppy needs to learn to trot alongside, allowing you to set the pace. Practice in your backyard from the day you bring your puppy home—that way, you'll have had a lot of practice walking together before going out and about when he finishes his vaccinations. Make sure you practice every day, and, as with all the other exercises, keep the sessions frequent and short—whatever you do with your dog when he's older is likely to involve leash walking, and if he's good at walking easily on a loose leash you'll have much more freedom in where you take him. Use a 6ft (1.8m) training leash to practice with; don't use an extendable leash. Most people opt to hold the leash in their right hand, and have the puppy walking on their left-hand side; this means they can hold a treat in the hand nearest the puppy for some extra persuasion when necessary.

1. Arm yourself with a pocketful of treats that are easily accessible. Clip the leash on your puppy's collar and hold it in your right hand, with a treat in your left hand.

2. Your puppy may wander around you at first. Make sure he knows where the treat is, and as soon as he's standing by your left side, give it to him and get another out. Feed him two or three treats as he's standing by your side. If he comes around to the front of you, lure him back into position with a treat. Don't start to walk until he's at your left side.

3. Holding a treat in your left hand, but this time up by your side where your puppy can smell it but can't reach it, say "Walk!" and walk forward just a couple of steps. Feed him the treat, get another ready in your hand, say "Walk!" and take another two steps.

4. At first this stop-go motion will feel very unnatural, but persist, ensuring that you have your puppy's focus each time before you start to walk. As you begin to move more easily together, add a step or two extra in between treats, praising him whenever he's moving alongside you easily with a loose leash.

5. At some point, your puppy will lose focus and start to walk away from you or across you. As the leash goes taut, hold it and make sure he remembers where the treats are. Don't walk around him or change the leash from hand to hand to get him back in the right position; let him work it out. As soon as he's back by your side, give him the treat, say "Walk!" and move off again.

BACKYARD PRACTICE

While your puppy is still at the early stages of leash walking, give him plenty of practice in the yard. Don't march round and round it in the same circle—go different ways, walk across it diagonally, take little circles around the outdoor furniture—even a small yard offers plenty of possibilities. Your puppy's job is to learn to stay by your side without pulling, so introduce as much variety as possible. Very gradually, as he gets more accomplished at anticipating your movements and shadowing you, still with a loose leash, leave slightly longer gaps between treats. Talking to him as you walk together will help to keep his attention on you.

PRACTICE OUTSIDE

Once he's had his final vaccination shot, you can take your puppy walking outside. Roads, people, traffic, and other dogs will all be hugely distracting at first, so keep the walks very short and be prepared to stop and start in a way you haven't had to since your very first walking-in-the-yard sessions. As usual with training, absolute consistency is crucial—you mustn't ever allow your puppy to pull on the leash just because you want to get somewhere, or he won't understand why he shouldn't do it the next time. If you don't have the time to train as you walk—if you're trying to get somewhere on a tight schedule, for instance—leave your puppy at home. For the first two or three months, every walk with your puppy will be a training walk.

HOW LONG SHOULD YOU TRAIN FOR?

If you're spending a few short sessions a day training your puppy, he will probably be getting the idea of the core things you need him to know by four months, be fairly reliable at six months, and solid by the time he gets to his first birthday. After that, the occasional session just as a reminder will be all you need. Sometimes you'll hit a period during his development when he seems to forget what he's learned, or seems unwilling to go along with things you thought he'd mastered. If this happens, be patient and keep up the regular short training sessions. The likelihood is that it's just a phase in his development as he's growing up and feeling more independent. If you stay calm and consistent, the training will come back as it passes.

TEACHING TRICKS

Even though they're not essential, it doesn't do any harm for your puppy to have a cute trick or two in his repertoire. "Shake hands" may win him an extra biscuit when you're out visiting, and "Rollover" is a guaranteed winner with small children. Some dogs are keener than others on learning tricks: if you've got a

natural show-off and you enjoy teaching him, your puppy will love the praise and laughter that each new performance brings.

TEACHING "SHAKE HANDS"

1. Start with your puppy in a sit. Take a treat and hold it in your closed hand, so he can smell it, but not see it.

2. Keep holding it near his nose, but don't open your hand. As he gets keener to get at it, he will paw at your hand to get it to open.

3. As he raises his paw to your hand, open your hand and give him the treat.

4. Repeat several times until he begins to connect raising his paw with getting the treat. Add the verbal cue, "Shake hands!" as his paw touches your hand, and just before you give him the treat.

Keep practicing until he's perfect every time before showing his new trick off to friends and family.

TEACHING "ROLLOVER"

You need your puppy to have learned "Down" before he can learn "Rollover." To rollover, he first needs to learn to roll onto his side, and then to go gradually further and further over until he's on his back with his feet in the air. It may take a number of sessions to get the full rollover, and it's often easiest to teach it in two parts—first to get him to lie on his side, and then, when he can do that, to use treats to entice him on to master the full roll.

1. Start with your puppy in the "Down" position.

2. Take a treat, hold it in front of him so he can smell it, then bring it slowly and gradually round the side of his face toward his shoulder. He'll turn his head to follow the treat and, as he does so, he will start to roll onto his side.

3. As soon as he's on his side, give him the treat.

4. Let him get up, then ask him to get back into a "Down," and repeat. Move the treat a tiny bit further round each time you practice—very gradually, lying on

his side will become lying on his back as he has to reach further to get the treat.

5. Add the verbal cue, "Rollover!" only after he's learned to lie on his side and is rolling slightly further over—say it as he rolls, and at the same moment that you give him the treat.

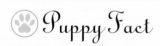

🐾 Puppy Fact

If your puppy has trouble learning a command and you're getting frustrated, don't prolong the session; it will actually slow the learning process down. Instead, set yourself up for success by going back to a command that you know he has mastered, so that you can end things on a positive note, and try again next time.

No. 16 PUPPY DEVELOPMENT

FROM EIGHT WEEKS TO ONE YEAR

*F*rom birth to a year old is a long time in a dog's life. Although the widely used general rule is that each "dog" year equates to seven in human terms, the journey to adulthood is a little more complicated than that. How quickly your dog matures depends on a number of factors. His breed is relevant: most large breeds mature more slowly than smaller ones, with giant breeds sometimes behaving in quite a puppy-like way until they are around two years old or even more. His character counts, too—all dogs are individuals and generalization works only up to a certain point; any trainer will tell you that within the same litter, you can have a sensible, early-maturing pup and a scattier sibling who shows markedly puppy-like behavior until he is much older. Despite this, every dog will go through a set of milestones in the course of his journey to adulthood.

KEEP A RECORD

A new puppy always features in casual snaps, but you can use photos to keep a slightly more formal record of how much he grows and changes through his first year with you. Take a photograph every week, in the same spot, with the same items around him, to give an idea of scale. At the end of a year, you'll have a scrapbook of pictures showing all the minute changes and advances he's made.

MILESTONES IN DEVELOPMENT

This chart shows the ways in which your puppy was affected by his surroundings from the very first day. It demonstrates the sheer speed at which puppies learn, and underlines why it's so important to get a puppy from a reputable breeder who has been careful to provide both mother and pups with the right sort of support up to the point at which you bring him home.

HOW OLD	HOW TO SUPPORT THE PUPPY
FROM BIRTH TO 12 DAYS • Puppies are born deaf and blind, but they can already smell, taste, and have their sense of touch. • They need stimulation to defecate. • They need to be kept warm, as they can't regulate their own body heat. • They are developing physically, but they aren't making connections away from their mother or consciously learning. Most of their energy is spent growing.	• The puppies' mother feeds them and keeps them warm. The litter will also lie together, warming one another with their bodies. Their mother will lick them all over, both to keep them clean and stimulate them to evacuate their body waste. This licking will be the puppy's first experience of comfort through touch. This is all the support or stimulation the puppies need for their first two weeks.

HOW OLD	HOW TO SUPPORT THE PUPPY

FROM TWO TO THREE WEEKS

- The puppies' eyes will open and their hearing will begin to operate.
- They begin to use their noses and respond to different smells.
- They are much more active and by the end of the third week will begin to play with one another.

- New sensations can be introduced to the puppies, such as different textures of cloth. Anything that stimulates their senses will help their development at this stage.
- The puppies should be handled gently for a few minutes each daily.

FROM THREE TO FOUR WEEKS

- Puppies begin to learn from their experiences.
- They are strongly bonded with their mother and siblings and become distressed if removed from them for any length of time.
- The "startle" reflex is developed; puppies will start at loud noises or sudden movements.
- Their sight and hearing are much stronger and more directed.
- Their communication skills start to develop—they will begin to bark and wag their tails, and can move their ears in the direction of sounds.
- Their awareness of their surroundings is much greater, and they absorb more lessons from their environment.

- The puppies' mother will usually have begun weaning at three to four weeks. Puppies can be offered mushy food from three weeks, and solid food by five weeks.
- Provide gentle background noise; avoid loud or sudden noises that will shock the puppies.
- Handle each puppy daily and give him a little time away from the litter—at between three and five weeks he will start to play with objects and to interact with people as well as with his mother and siblings.
- Introduce different objects into the puppy pen and allow the puppies limited exploration time outside it.
- Make a division between areas within the puppy pen or introduce an activity or play area outside it.

HOW OLD	HOW TO SUPPORT THE PUPPY

FROM FIVE TO SEVEN WEEKS

- By seven weeks, the puppies will usually be fully weaned.
- Puppies will spend more time playing with their siblings.
- They will play-fight and their bite inhibition will develop quickly.
- Their physical coordination strengthens daily.
- The key socialization period has begun.
- Puppies will show an increasing degree of independence.

- Engineer plenty of stage-managed, gentle and positive encounters with new people.
- Give puppies short periods on their own to help to prepare them for separation from their mother and littermates.
- Start active play with puppies, using small food treats and toys.

FROM EIGHT TO 12 WEEKS

- At eight weeks, the puppy will usually be taken to his new home.
- He'll be taking on board completely new surroundings and people.
- The period at which he learns fastest has begun and will continue to around four months.
- He may become easily fearful about new experiences (this is known as a Fear Impact period) and needs careful introductions to ensure his experiences are positive.

- Don't expect too much of him for the first week or two.
- Offer plenty of gently managed new experiences, such as car rides or encounters with unfamiliar people.
- Start housetraining. By eight weeks, puppies have the bowel and bladder control to "hold" for short periods.
- Start obedience training: train little and often.
- Start crate training, and ensure the puppy has short periods alone. The sooner he's accustomed to being on his own, the less likely he is to suffer from separation anxiety later on.

HOW OLD	HOW TO SUPPORT THE PUPPY

FROM 12 TO 16 WEEKS

- By the four-month milestone a puppy's brain is three-quarters of the way to its full adult development.
- From around three months old, he'll be experimenting to find his place in "his" pack, and trying out different behaviors.
- From the end of this period, his chewing will be almost constant as his second set of teeth begins to develop.

- Provide plenty of positive exercises to use his mental energy usefully.
- Offer suitable chews and chew toys—and make sure that anything that shouldn't be chewed is out of reach.
- Use training to establish your role as his leader, and the head of his particular pack.

FROM FOUR TO SIX MONTHS

- The early intense learning period comes to an end.
- The puppy has more stamina; the days when he simply keels over and falls asleep, mid-activity, are coming to a close.
- Another intensive growth spurt: by six months, he'll probably have grown his adult coat and be reaching adult height.
- He may have a second Fear Impact period (he becomes exaggeratedly reactive to unfamiliar things). This usually arrives in the fifth month and may last two to four weeks.

- Continue steady, consistent training and socialization.
- Take particular care if he becomes fearful in new situations; reassurance and support can help to counter his instinctive reactions, and the more stage-managed new encounters are, the more able you will be to ensure a positive outcome.
- Continue to reinforce all good behavior strongly—this will help as he reaches the six-month milestone.

HOW OLD	HOW TO SUPPORT THE PUPPY

FROM SIX TO EIGHT MONTHS

- The puppy begins to reach sexual maturity and may start exhibiting signs of sexual behavior such as humping.
- There may be occasions when he challenges the status quo.
- Things you thought he had learned long ago—such as recall—may become patchy.
- His response to other dogs may become barky or defensive, particularly if he didn't experience full-on socialization earlier on in puppyhood.

- Go back to the beginning with training exercises if he seems to have forgotten the basics.
- Be patient with adolescent "posturing": he's simply trying out his place in the world.
- If you are going to neuter or spay, discuss the best timetable with your vet.
- Keep up his socialization with other known and trusted adult dogs.

FROM EIGHT MONTHS TO A YEAR

- Adolescence will continue through much of this period.
- His chewing will still be an issue—and his jaws will become more powerful.
- His rate of growth (depending on his breed) may start to slow down as he reaches his year milestone—although larger breeds will still have some growing to do.
- He may show some guarding behavior over food and toys.

- Continue to train and reinforce consistently. Increase the number of training sessions if necessary, but keep them short.
- Make sure there are enough heavy-duty toys and bones to manage his need to chew.
- Establish swapping and resource exchange as a regular part of his training to manage any tendency to guard.

No. 17 BATHING AND GROOMING

KEEPING YOUR PUPPY CLEAN

clean, well-groomed puppy is nicer to live with than a dirty one, and the earlier you accustom your pet to being bathed and brushed the easier you'll find keeping up the routine when he's an adult. A grooming session is also an opportunity for an all-round body check, so even if your puppy has an easy-care coat, aim to give him a thorough brush a couple of times a week. Bathing can happen on a when he-needs-it basis—which, given many puppies' propensity for digging or rolling in anything unsavory they can find, may be rather more often than you'd like. Whether you're grooming or bathing your puppy, keep up a reassuring stream of chat, pitching your voice low, and making sure that you sound calm and cheerful. When the session is finished, give him a treat and play with him for a minute or two, to leave him with as positive an impression of the whole experience as possible.

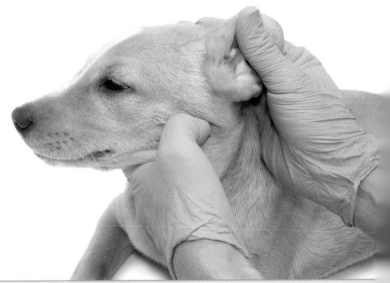

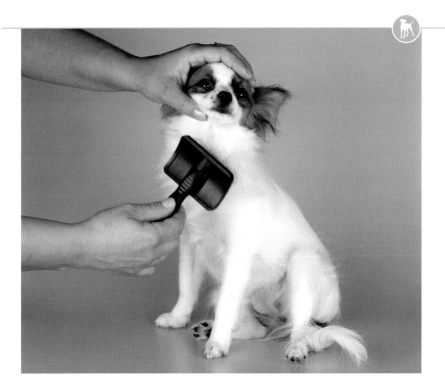

COAT CARE

If your puppy came from a breeder, check with them how they care for their dogs' coats to keep them in top condition. Care levels vary a good deal, with a long, silky coat taking a lot more time than the short, easy-brush type. Even the shortest coats need regular brushing—it gets rid of shed hairs and distributes the oils in the hair evenly across the coat, which helps to keep it in good condition. And even dogs famous for having "non-shed" coats need grooming—they *do* shed, just less evidently and copiously than other breeds. Some types of coat will need regular clipping as well as bathing and grooming.

COAT TYPES

The main division in coat types is whether or not your puppy has a single or a double coat. A double coat consists of a top coat, a layer of relatively coarse hairs known as guard hairs, and a softer, fluffier undercoat. A single coat means that the dog has the top coat only. Whether or not a coat is single or double depends on your puppy's breed and parentage, and isn't affected by how long the coat is—a long-haired dog may still be single-coated, while a short-haired one may have a double coat. Finally, there's the question of coat texture, which in dogs ranges from very soft and silky to quite rough and harsh.

WHAT YOU NEED

For the first few sessions of grooming, use only a soft bristle brush (sometimes marketed as a puppy brush) until your puppy is used to the sensation of being brushed. A pin brush, which has wire "bristles" topped with soft rubber tips, can also be useful—it brushes without pulling too much and too uncomfortably at the coat. A wide-toothed comb will help you to work out tangles gently, too.

STARTING OUT
Your puppy's first grooming session

As usual with any new experiences, keep some of his favorite treats at hand; they'll help to persuade him that grooming is an enjoyable process.

- Keep your first sessions of grooming very short—a minute of gentle brushing is plenty. That way, he's likely to see it as just another cuddle. You can gradually increase the time you spend brushing him as your puppy gets used to it.
- Groom when the puppy has just had a vigorous play session and a trip outside: if he's tired and doesn't need to toilet, he's more likely to accept the grooming happily.
- Get down to the puppy's level to groom him. There's no need to place him on a table or other high surface, and he'll be more relaxed if he's on the ground.
- Place your puppy on an old piece of towel or cloth to groom; this will catch any stray hairs or dander from his coat and you can shake it outside and then wash it when the grooming session is finished.
- Use the grooming session to check your puppy all over—you'll get used to how he feels and will soon be able to spot any potential problems as you groom: unfamiliar lumps and bumps, any bites or cuts under his coat that you've overlooked, grass seeds creating knots between his toes, and so on. A good, thorough brush can also act as a regular health check.
- If the puppy keeps wriggling and trying to get away when you're brushing him, stop brushing and gently hold him still. The moment he quietens down and stops squirming, let him go and give him a treat. This teaches him that he'll be released if he's calm.

As your puppy gets used to being groomed, you can concentrate more on the actual process and less on his reaction to it. A good grooming session can also be a bonding time between you, leaving your puppy feeling comfortable, soothed and clean.

- Start with the areas of his body that most dogs aren't too sensitive about—his back and his sides.
- Brush his back smoothly from the nape to the area above his tail, working in the direction his coat grows in. Use a soft brush that won't get stuck in any knots or snarls if he has a long coat.
- When you feel the brush going over a tangle, go back over the area and locate it. Separate it out with your fingers, then separate the strands of hair, first with your fingers and then with a wide-toothed comb. Gradually work through the clump until the knot has gone. Never just pull on the brush if there's a knot; it will pull directly on the skin and hurt the puppy.
- After you've brushed all down the puppy's back, start on his sides. Lure him onto his side with a treat if necessary.

- Work gradually around his ribs until you can brush his belly. Many dogs are quite sensitive about this area, so work gradually, and use the brush and comb gently.
- Now brush around his neck. In double-coated breeds, the hair in this area tends to be very thick. Work slowly.
- Finally, gently brush his paws and tail. Most dogs are fussy about letting anyone touch their paws, so take one paw at a time, separate out the toes and look for any knots or lumps, then comb carefully through the hair on the top and back of the paw. It's usually easier to brush a puppy's tail when he's standing up, so lure him into a standing position with a treat, then place a hand under his chest to hold him in place while you comb gently through his tail.

Examining his ears and mouth

- At the end of a grooming session, look inside your puppy's ears and mouth.
- Raise the flap of each ear; the inside should look clean and be pale pink, without a lot of wax or any dirty discharge or inflammation. Don't ever try to clean inside your puppy's ears yourself: if they look dirty or inflamed, take him to the vet.
- Raise his lip gently with your thumb and run it around his teeth. This is just to get your puppy used to allowing you to look inside his mouth; the first step toward him allowing you to brush his teeth.

THE HARD STUFF
Brushing your puppy's teeth

If you decide to brush your puppy's teeth you're setting him up for a lifetime of good dental hygiene and you may be saving yourself a fortune in doggy dental appointments later on. While there's not a huge practical benefit in brushing his puppy teeth (he'll be losing them anyway before long), the sooner you get him used to the procedure, the easier you'll find it as his adult teeth come in and his jaws become more powerful.

You can either use a child's toothbrush or a special puppy toothbrush. Buy some toothpaste manufactured for dogs (you can find this at the pet shop or online). Some toothpastes are flavored with meat or cheese to make them more appealing to your puppy—unlike you, he won't spit, so he'll be swallowing the paste residue. The more intriguing he finds the flavor, the easier you're likely to find it to brush his teeth.

- Put a little paste on the brush, and add water so that it's easily worked into a froth.

 Puppy Fact

It's only worth brushing your puppy's teeth if you're prepared to do it every day. Research has shown that dogs' dental health was positively affected if their teeth were brushed once a day, but that the benefits became negligible if this was reduced to just two or three times a week.

- Holding your puppy, gently raise his upper gum away from his teeth and brush along the top teeth. Repeat with the lower gum and the lower teeth.
- Keep brushing very brief at first—just one or two forward-and-back motions with the brush should be enough to get your puppy used to the idea without frightening him.
- If the puppy tries to chew the brush, take it away and try again a minute or two later. When he's calmly accepting a short tooth-cleaning session, finish it by praising and treating him.

Clipping your puppy's nails

Older dogs who are walked a lot, especially on hard surfaces, don't always need their nails clipped (although some do), but puppies have very fine, pointed toenails that have extremely sharp ends that do usually need trimming every month or two. You can either ask the vet to clip them at one of your puppy's early appointments or you can do it yourself using nail clippers. Most dogs don't enjoy having their nails clipped, so if you decide to do it yourself, keep your movements confident and ask someone else to help you hold the puppy and soothe it while you're doing the clipping.

Err on the side of caution—if your puppy has dark nails it can be hard to see where the "quick" (the part of the nail that attaches to the paw pad) of each nail starts, and if you cut into the quick with the clippers, it can bleed surprisingly heavily. Make sure the clippers are sharp, clip only the outmost point of the nail, and if your puppy is becoming distressed after you've clipped a paw, praise and treat him and set up a second session a few hours later to finish the job—don't insist on doing all four paws in one go.

BATHTIME

Bathing a puppy is much easier if you set up everything easily within reach before you start.

What you need:

- A non-slip mat for the bathtub or sink. Your puppy will be much less nervous if his feet aren't slipping around as you bath him.
- A plastic jug with a weak dilution of shampoo in tepid water. You can use either special dog shampoo or a baby shampoo.
- Either another plastic jug (for getting the puppy wet before you lather him up) or a spray attachment for the faucet/s.
- Plenty of towels, both for lifting your puppy out of the bathtub and for drying him off when he's out.

If you're using a spray attachment, get the temperature of the water right before putting your puppy in the bathtub. It should be warm, not hot—blood heat or just slightly warmer. If you're not using a spray attachment, put the plug in the tub and run 2–3in (5–7cm) of tepid water into the bathtub, so that you can use a jug to scoop up water and pour it over your puppy.

How to bath a puppy

- Lay the non-slip mat on the floor of the bath or sink.
- Pick the puppy up gently and put him on the mat. Talk to him soothingly all the time that you're bathing him to keep him from getting too nervous.
- Either using the spray set to a gentle setting or the plastic jug, wet the puppy all over, pouring water over him slowly and carefully. Aim the spray away from his eyes, down his back. Make sure he's thoroughly wet all over (some puppy's coats are water-repellent, so it takes a minute or two to get them wet to the skin).
- Slowly pour some of the shampoo solution over the puppy and begin to lather him up. Be careful washing around his neck and the top of his head and make sure you don't get any soap in his eyes. If the fur under his eyes is dirty or has any residue from discharge, use the corner of a damp cloth, very delicately, to wipe it away.
- When you've soaped him all over, use the jug or the spray to rinse the soap off him. If he has a long coat, wring it out with your hands to make sure you've removed all the soap.
- When he's been thoroughly rinsed and is clean, pull the plug out of the bathtub or sink, let the water run away, and squeeze your puppy's coat a little to get rid of as much of the water as you can.
- Drape a towel over the puppy while he's

still in the bathtub, and wrap it around him to lift him out and onto another towel spread on the floor.

• His immediate reaction will be to shake himself dry, so keep him wrapped in the towel for a minute or two—he can shake himself inside it. Gently rub him dry through the towel until he's no longer very wet. Change the towel for a dry one if you need to.

As soon as he's reasonably dry, remove the towels. He'll shake himself violently, and, straight out of the bathtub, most puppies will do a mad five-minute dash around the house. It's amusing to watch (and will help him to dry off) but if you don't want him spraying water all over the place, it makes sense to get him as dry as possible before you let him go. If you want to avoid any mess altogether, carry him out to the backyard in his towel and let him have his mad five minutes out there.

Unless he has a very heavy coat, you probably won't need to dry him beyond this (and after a minute or two's dash about, most puppies will find a warm place to finish drying off), but if he has a long or high-maintenance coat, you may need to use a hairdryer. It's best to have introduced him to this as part of his socialization process before you use it to dry him—both the noise it makes and the way it blows out hot air may frighten a nervous puppy and the first time he

sees it, it certainly shouldn't be aimed directly at him. Whether you towel him dry or use a hairdryer, make sure he doesn't get cold while he's still damp—keep him somewhere warm until he's completely dry. If your puppy seems worried by the whole bathing routine and the weather is mild enough, you can bathe him out of doors instead, in a large plastic bowl of tepid water. Sometimes being outside and feeling less confined seems to help more timid dogs to accept the whole process.

CLIPPING

Some puppies' coats need clipping or other specialist grooming as well as washing. Specific breeds of Terrier, for example, may need their coats "stripped" out. It's best to turn to the professionals to do this—a home-done clip usually yields a very amateur-looking result. Ask among dog-owning friends for a recommendation for a good groomer—some will make home visits, which can be more reassuring for your puppy, while others will let you stay with your dog while he is groomed.

WATCHING YOUR PUPPY MATURE

t about six months old, adolescence kicks in for most dogs. Small dogs tend to mature slightly earlier and large ones slightly later, but at some point around this age you will start to notice changes in your pet. Male dogs will begin to cock their legs when they pee; female dogs will come into season for the first time. And some personality changes will usually arrive along with the physical ones.

This section looks at the changes you can expect to see in your dog, while the next one offers some ways in which you can troubleshoot problems as your mischievous but essentially biddable puppy turns into a canine teenager. Your pet may want to test the boundaries and, while you're probably not having small-puppy issues like constant housetraining accidents any more, you may find that he's easily distracted, seems to "forget" training that you thought was established weeks ago, and generally starts to try out a more independent approach to life. Add to this the fact that your pet is attaining their sexual maturity, and you're likely to find that you have a challenge on your hands for a few more months.

IS IT HIM OR YOU?

Estimated percentages vary, but it's a sad fact that the vast majority of dogs who are given up to shelters in both the US and the UK are surrendered at between eight months and two years old. And it's also during pets' adolescence that professional trainers or behaviorists are most often called in to deal with problems. The shelter or trainer is frequently told that the dog is too energetic, is taking up far too much time, or even that it is out of control.

BEHIND THE SIGNS

When Will My Puppy Be "Grown Up?"

That depends on his size and breed, and all breeders and experts agree that it can depend on the individual dog as well, so the answer can only be approximate. In general, though, the larger the dog, the slower he is to reach full maturity. A small Terrier, for example, is usually at his adult size by the time he's a year old and may be emerging from adolescence, while a larger dog, such as a Labrador, may not reach its full size (or start to adopt a more grown-up attitude) until he is 18 months or even two years old.

If, at between six and eight months old, your dog is proving more demanding than expected, ask yourself the following:

1. IS HE GETTING ENOUGH EXERCISE?

Young puppies play all day and, with all the growing and learning they're doing, they're usually tired at the end of it. They don't really need long or formal walks. A teenage dog needs more planned exercise, whether it's an hour of off-leash walking or a tiring play either with other dogs or with "his" people. If your dog loves to retrieve a ball or enjoys a game of football, it will tire him out more thoroughly than any amount of on-leash walking. Don't overdo it, though—for the first year, your pet's muscles and bones are still developing and he shouldn't undertake long runs; if you want a jogging buddy, wait a few months, and if he looks tired, call a halt to play and give him a break. Try to keep his exercise varied as well as energetic, so you tire out his mind as well as his body. And don't forget that he needs exercise every day, not just at weekends, so that his stamina builds gradually—steady and regular is the key here.

2. ARE YOU KEEPING UP HIS TRAINING?

If you thought "He's got it!" at four months, and then let the training slip a little, now is the time to reintroduce several short sessions a day. As with younger puppies, little and often is still the rule, with plenty

There are certainly all kinds of reasons for the problem. But most trainers believe that the owners of adolescent dogs weren't well enough prepared for what a challenge this stage might be. Certainly, the answer to many concerns around the behavior of a teenage dog is simply to step up his training.

When you brought your puppy home, you knew that he represented a big commitment in time and energy and you were probably prepared to take plenty of time to housebreak and socialize him. Unfortunately, the teenage puppy stage is less familiar; many people wrongly assume that, once the first stage of puppyhood is over, so is the hard work. As he grows and becomes an accepted part of the household, too, he will inevitably lose some of his novelty value. But the teenage months probably call for more patience and consistency than the early months did.

of rewards when he gets it right. Ideally, training should be kept up all the way into adulthood, with games and challenges introduced to keep well-worn routines fresh.

3. ARE YOU KEEPING UP HIS SOCIALIZATION?

It's as important as it ever was that you keep introducing him to all sorts of varied experiences while he's still young. Just because the key socialization window ends at around 16 weeks, it doesn't mean that you should stop taking him around and spending dedicated time keeping up his social skills—they will always need reinforcing regularly. Because most dogs have a second "fear" period at five or six months of age (when you may notice an increased reaction to new things, and sometimes an exaggerated caution towards them), it's especially important that this is worked through with consistency and plenty of exposure to different situations.

4. ARE YOU REMEMBERING TO REINFORCE GOOD BEHAVIOR AND IGNORE BEHAVIOR YOU DON'T WANT?

Adolescent dogs are experts at pushing your buttons. It's crucial that you remember the basics. If your teenage puppy has just spent five minutes ignoring you when you called him back in the park, it can be tempting to shout at him when he finally bounds cheerfully over. Don't do it: even if it's through gritted teeth, praise and treat him—trust is more important than ever at this stage in your relationship. Keeping up his routines and regularly reminding him that you are his pack leader and it's through you that all the good things happen will pay off in the end.

If you keep all these factors in mind, engage with your puppy enthusiastically and consistently, and remember to give him plenty of praise when he does get it right, you'll come through the teenage months with your bond stronger than ever.

Rebellious, Or Under-trained?

Unfortunately no definitive research has been carried out on adolescence in dogs, so the various behavioral theories aren't supported by hard evidence. Some experts believe that at least some of the changes that owners report result from dogs simply becoming larger and harder to ignore or control. A little puppy that jumps up on visitors may still seem cute, but a large teenage dog that knocks over an elderly caller won't be looked on with the same indulgence. Keep this in mind, and make sure that behavioral challenges aren't simply the result of a more casual approach to training on your part.

RELATIONSHIPS WITH OTHER DOGS

One thing that you may notice as your dog emerges from puppyhood is that his relationships with other dogs begin to change. When a puppy reaches five or six months, older dogs will start to treat him as an adult and behavior that might have been acceptable when he was very small will begin to be corrected in an adult way. Add to this the fact that hormonal changes may mean that both dogs and bitches become more "full on" with their encounters with other dogs, and playtime with others becomes especially important. If you can, during this period, try to pick his playmates from the well-adjusted adult dogs you know. Most of them will deal with a pestering or ill-mannered teenager with a short, sharp correction: typically an explosion of snapping or growling, with plenty of teeth on display and no harm done. Provided that your pet is getting plenty of playtime with familiar dogs who you know to be generally good tempered and fairly tolerant, it's best to allow them to sort it out between themselves without any interference. It is important that he learn his place in the local dog hierarchy, and these corrections, although they can sound scary to humans, are simply reminders that he isn't a baby any longer and needs to show respect to his elders and act his age. A well-socialized puppy who has mixed with plenty of other dogs will "read" the message correctly and will soon learn to rein in his overexuberance.

WHEN SHOULD YOU NEUTER?

If you're not planning on breeding from your pet, the subject of neutering will arise as your dog turns teenage. Dogs who are not bred from are at risk from certain conditions associated with their reproductive systems, and there's also the question of accidental pregnancies—which are commoner than you might think. So if you don't want puppies, it is probably better and safer overall to neuter.

There are a lot of theories about the best age to carry out neutering, with the general current practice being to operate relatively young, usually at the six-month point or even earlier, while bitches are generally spayed shortly after their first season. Advocates of early neutering for both sexes argue that the younger the operation is performed the less disruptive it is physically for the dog; the counterargument is that unless dogs are given the opportunity to mature sexually, they haven't produced enough of either the crucial thyroid hormones, or testosterone (in the case of dogs) or estrogen (in the case of bitches) to grow and mature properly. All these hormones begin to be produced at the point at which your puppy attains sexual maturity, and are considered to be important in supporting the immune system, as well ensuring overall health and growth (in particular, healthy bone

development), so it's important that puppies produce enough of them to have the necessary effects before being neutered. The breed of your dog may affect the age he or she should be neutered, since larger breeds are generally slower to reach maturity than smaller ones. With all these factors to be taken into consideration with your own pet, you should take expert advice. Ask your vet's opinion about what the right age will be to neuter or spay for your own dog, and why.

Both operations need a general anesthetic and your dog will need to take it easy for a few days afterward, so if you plan to neuter, arrange for the operation to happen at a quiet time when he or she can have company at home, you can ensure that they aren't interfering with their wound stitches, and the house isn't too busy and is peaceful enough for them to recuperate. Young dogs usually recover quite quickly from neutering or spaying and within a week or so will be running around as usual.

NEW ACTIVITIES?

Even if your puppy adores his exercise regime as it is, adolescence is a good time to introduce some fresh activities to his timetable. If he attended puppy parties when he was smaller, he may enjoy some organized social fun, or it may be time for his first group training class. Check out what's available locally at your vet's surgery or with other dog owners.

Training classes

Many trainers run special "adolescent" classes specifically for puppies of around six months or a little over. These have the advantage that your dog will be mixing with others close to his own age, and it's a chance for him to be around other dogs while retaining his focus on you. Make sure before you join that the class uses methods based on positive reinforcement and not punishment; ask if you can attend one class without your puppy to see how it works and ensure it teaches in a way you'll both be happy with. When you do take him along, be ready to have your puppy apparently forget everything he knows for the first class or two as he overexcitedly checks out his classmates and his new surroundings.

For a more mixed experience, most trainers are also happy for you to take a six-months-plus puppy along to a general training class. You'll probably find a mixed bunch of dogs attending this for different reasons, from help with socialization to a refresher for their obedience.

All training classes have the primary aim of getting dogs to pay attention to their owners, so whichever you choose, it will support the training you're doing at home.

Social dog walking groups

A movement growing in popularity, these groups get together a number of like-minded dog owners, sometimes with a trainer, sometimes without, and practice on-leash walking, and sometimes other exercises too, out of doors. Those groups that are led by a trainer often incorporate a variety of small obedience or agility exercises within the class (these can be as simple as hopping on and off a bench in exchange for a treat); others may simply concentrate on an on-leash walk of a mile or two, with dogs walking side-by-side. If your dog seems to have become shyer or very assertive as he's hit the six-month milestone, social walking can help his socialization skills in a friendly, not-too-structured environment and introduce him to a number of new dogs without placing too much expectation on his shoulders. Look online for local groups and check out the rules before you join—some include some off-leash time in the course of the walk, others offer walks of varying length (some of which may be too long for a puppy), and so on—every group is different.

WHAT TO LOOK OUT FOR IN A TRAINING CLASS

A good class:
- should have an easy, calm atmosphere without any feeling of stress;
- should have dogs who are at around the same level of learning/ training—most teenage dogs will do best in a beginner class;
- should teach with the aid of treats or toys;
- should feature games and exercises which involve everyone and every dog, with assistants to give individual help if needed;
- should be fairly small—around ten dogs is usually the maximum for an effective class.

Avoid any class in which:
- puppies are forcibly coerced into doing anything—in particular, avoid a class where any old-style owner "domination" tactics, such as pinning your puppy down to force obedience, are recommended;
- the teacher recommends electric, choke, or pinch collars or any other aversive treatment;
- owners are made to feel uncomfortable if their puppy isn't learning quickly or is disruptive within the class—it's all part of the learning process, and the teacher should be able to cope with canine adolescents (and their sometimes nervous owners).

KEEPING YOUR PUPPY BUSY

As well as out-of-the-house activities, teach him some new things at home. At the end of chapter 15, a couple of tricks were suggested to teach your puppy as a part of his training—if he was keen on these, you could experiment with one or two more complicated group games involving several people interacting with him. Most dogs love being part of a game and figuring out their role in it. Working out the rules is good mental exercise, too.

Hide and Go Seek

This is exactly the same game you might play with a small child. Hold your dog on a leash while someone else goes and hides. You could have them go out into the backyard and simply stand behind a tree at first, then ask them to choose more complicated hiding places as your puppy gets the hang of it. When the hider has taken up position (out of sight of both you and the dog), ask him in a high, excited voice, "Where's X?" Pretend to look with him, racing round and looking in one or two places X isn't, before discovering X with great fanfare and excitement. If there are several of you, you could have two different people hide, then help your puppy hunt them out one by one.

Find the Treat

This one is self-explanatory—have someone keep your puppy outside a closed door while you hide a dozen small treats around the room inside. Then open the door and invite your puppy to "find the treat." You're encouraging him to use his nose and he has the excitement of uncovering a succession of tasty treats. Pick a room where you won't mind a lot of frantic scrabbling and "digging" as he rummages for the food.

Build on What He Knows

The more a puppy learns, the easier he will find it to learn more. This applies both to formal training exercises and games—he won't differentiate between them. If you're finding training a strain as he tries out his new sense of independence, mix up obedience exercises with fun games like those on the left—after a session that, to him, simply consists of fun and treats, you may find it easier to engage him with "sit" and "stay" again.

MEETING THE CHALLENGES OF
AN ADOLESCENT DOG

*E*ven if you've followed all the advice and done everything right, most adolescent dogs will raise a few concerns at some point in their first year. This section looks at a handful of common problems and how to handle them. Even if your puppy does something that provokes or worries you, always react calmly—he needs to know that you're confident and in control even if, at some moments, you don't feel it. Although there will be times when it seems that your pet has forgotten all his training, don't worry: if you were consistent in teaching it, it's still there somewhere—it's just been temporarily pushed to the back of his teenage brain, ready to resurface when he's a little more grown up. In the meantime, though, you need to remind him and keep reminding him what you know he learned, and perhaps add some new ideas as a few new challenges arise.

GOING BACK TO THE BEGINNING

Whenever you hit a wall with your adolescent dog's behavior, take a few minutes to go right back to the very beginning—with a sit and stay. He knows how to do them, it's a calming exercise for both of you and running through a routine you both know keeps things simple and reestablishes your relative positions as teacher and pupil.

KEEPING IT WORTHWHILE

As your puppy became more accomplished in training you probably moved to occasional treats rather than rewarding him every time. Now that he's an adolescent, if his learning seems to have regressed a little, go back to the bonus-every-time-he-gets-it-right system

for a few weeks. Abandon any idea that he "should" have mastered the basics by now—you'd probably cut a human teenager some slack, so do the same with your canine equivalent, and make things as easy on him as you can. If you'd given up the habit of always having treats in your pocket as your puppy gradually seemed to be getting the hang of his training, take it up again, so you've always got a reward to hand; positive reinforcement is as important now as it was then.

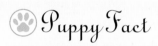

Puppy Fact

Your puppy is a social animal and, as such, he hates to be ignored. Withdrawing your attention is a very effective way to reform his behavior without damaging his trust in you. Old-style aversive punishments— shouting at, or even smacking a puppy—were undesirable not only because they were ineffective (because the puppy didn't make the connection between his own behavior and your reaction) and unkind, but also because they could result in fearful dog.

COMMON PROBLEMS

JUMPING UP

Perhaps you dealt with jumping up when he was a small puppy but it's started again, or maybe you never quite stopped him but now that he's (at least) twice the size, it's becoming a real problem.

WHAT TO DO

If your puppy jumps up for attention, you have to change his focus, deny him the attention, and reward him for doing something else. Make jumping up unrewarding by turning your body away from him as he jumps, and make sure everyone else in the household follows suit. Don't acknowledge the jumping in any way, or you'll be effectively "rewarding" him with your attention. Instead, turn your whole upper body away from him, and cross your arms. Most puppies will be surprised by this, and many will respond by sitting down. Even if he doesn't, he's unlikely to try to jump again. The moment his feet are on the floor, turn back, praise, and treat him. As usual, good timing is key. If everyone consistently reacts in the same way every time he jumps up, he should soon give it up.

NIPPING

Nipping was probably a feature of playing with your puppy when he was small, and it sometimes makes an unwelcome reappearance around the five- or six-month point. Now that your puppy is acquiring his adult teeth, it hurts a lot more, too; it's a habit that you must stop completely before he gets any older.

WHAT TO DO

Much like jumping up, the most effective way to stop your puppy nipping you is to refuse to engage. The moment he nips, say "ouch!" loudly, then get up and walk straight out of the room. Don't say anything else and don't make eye contact as you go. Make sure that everyone else who's around him regularly does exactly the same thing. If he follows you and tries to get your attention, ignore him for another minute or so (a minute is quite a long time for a puppy), then reengage with him in a positive way, by doing a training exercise or playing with a toy together.

REFUSING TO COME BACK

Small puppies tend to want to stay around you, and if you got used to your pet always being nearby you may not have practiced distance recall as regularly as some other exercises. His newfound independence will come as an unwelcome surprise—and loss of recall is very common in adolescent dogs. Suddenly everything is more interesting than coming back when you call: a new smell, a game of ball, another dog in the distance, or simply playing with his friends. Of all the challenges his teenagerhood offers, this can be the most exasperating to deal with.

WHAT TO DO

Try not to get into the habit of calling your puppy repeatedly if he's at some distance from you and not responding. If he doesn't respond to your first call of "Come!" walk over much nearer to him and try again. If he still doesn't respond, you may need to use a long line when you're out and he's playing so that you can actually get him back while you're retraining him in recall. Leave it trailing while he's running freely, but if he doesn't respond when you call, move nearer and step on one end of it before calling again. The slight restraint as he's brought up short may be enough to catch his attention and get him to respond to you. If it isn't, don't use it to pull him around, just walk up until you're close enough to put him on his walking leash. Then reintroduce recall exercises lots of times, every day, whatever you're both doing and in all sorts of surroundings.

Set yourself up to win by practicing when there are no other distractions around at first, gradually building up through various degrees of distraction. Above all, remember to praise him whenever he does come back, even if he doesn't always come immediately at first. Remember, too, the final step of touching his collar that you used when you were first teaching him, even when you're calling him across a very short distance—often in the future, you'll be calling him to put his leash on, and you want him to learn to stay still for that final step.

SHYNESS/FEAR

A puppy that was slightly shy and backhanging when he was small will sometimes begin to be fearful or snappy when meeting unfamiliar things or people as he reaches adolescence. This is usually the result of insufficiently broad socialization when he was younger, and needs very careful handling.

WHAT TO DO
Take a two-pronged approach to stop it turning into a serious concern. You need to broaden your puppy's socialization without increasing his fear. At the same time, you need to reinforce his perception of you as pack leader, because it makes it more likely that he will rely on you to deal with situations that frighten him, rather than feeling that it's up to him to do so. Spend the time necessary on dealing with this—shortcomings in socialization must be made up for while your pet is still young, so that his fearful responses don't become a habit. Don't wrap your puppy in

cotton wool or shut him away from new situations, but as far as possible stage-manage his introductions to anything new. At the same time, go back a step or two in his training, with plenty of short, easy sessions and games to reinforce things he already knows—this will help to build his confidence and encourage him to trust you to lead him through situations that are less familiar.

If he responds to something new with fear, calmly take him out of the situation—forcing him to confront something he's afraid of at this stage is likely to make him think he needs to defend himself from whatever he's frightened of. Maintain his socialization, but take care to ensure he never feels overwhelmed, and as far as possible manage new situations—for example, set up playdates with older dogs you know to be calm and friendly rather than taking him to the park and seeing who he meets up with.

AGGRESSION TOWARDS OTHER DOGS

If your puppy suddenly develops snappiness around new canine acquaintances, it may be his hormones talking. As dogs grow into sexual maturity and they lose the license that adult dogs usually extend to small puppies, they can become uncertain of how to respond when they're meeting and greeting new dogs. Males may try to mount unfamiliar dogs or demonstrate rather uptight, aggressive-looking stances (standing tall and showing unusually still/rigid body language are typical); females may object to being sniffed by unknown dogs, even if they're obviously friendly. Both sexes may get into scraps with dogs they don't know, which can be unnerving for you as owner, even if they're characterized more by noise than anything more serious.

WHAT TO DO

Just like visible timidity, aggression in a maturing puppy is often fear-based. Whatever you do, don't avoid other dogs—your pet needs socialization more than ever at this stage. Mature, calm dogs will usually cope with a posturing teenager without the situation escalating into something unmanageable, so follow the same rules as you would with a puppy who is evidently shy and fearful: arrange meet-ups and walks with dogs you know to be "safe," and try out some social situations in which your dog is under no social pressure—for example, you might take your puppy on an on-leash walk with a sociable older dog, so that they can walk parallel to one another and have limited contact, but your puppy has no need to feel he has to "manage" the situation.

CALLING IN THE PROFESSIONALS

If you feel that you've tried everything and that you still need some extra assistance, there's no shame in asking for professional help. There are plenty of trainers and behaviorists out there, and one of them will be right for you and will be able to help you with your puppy. In particular if you are having a problem with your puppy's shyness or aggression and are feeling that you can't cope, it's best to seek help sooner rather than later so that the problem behavior doesn't have time to become an established habit.

What's the difference between a trainer and a behaviorist?

A trainer is usually someone who will give your puppy obedience training, one-to-one, and show you what to do to get your dog to do what you ask. You might call them in if you simply can't get your adolescent puppy to walk on leash, or if he refuses to come back when called, however much training you've done. A behaviorist is someone who looks at the root cause of a problem, and is more likely to be called in for issues like separation anxiety, or fear-based aggression, when your puppy is reacting in a way you don't altogether understand and you don't know what to do about it. Neither should ever use or suggest methods that are based on anything but positive reinforcement.

If you decide that you need help, do plenty of research into who could be right for you and your dog. This isn't a well-regulated field, so a recommendation from a vet or from someone you trust who has a lot of animal experience is the best way to go, and the specialist you consult should have plenty of demonstrable experience of their own. They should be happy to meet you on your own and answer any questions you have before arranging a meeting with you and your puppy, and most will want to ask a number of questions of their own before either meeting you or making any recommendations. Follow your feelings on whether they are "right" for you—you must be comfortable with their methods and they should be respectful of both you and your puppy's comfort levels if you're going to work well together.

PRACTICE, PRACTICE, PRACTICE

Reinforcement training is the key to getting your dog through the trickier moments of his adolescence. Most problems can be overcome by simply going back to training basics and practicing them together again and again. Keep the exercises fresh with plenty of play breaks and treats, and even at down moments, maintain an upbeat, cheerful tone. Even a wilful adolescent dog needs leadership, and the work will pay off as he emerges from this final stage of his puppyhood with both his training and his relationship with you intact.

LOOKING INTO THE FUTURE

t some point between the end of his first year and hitting his 18-month milestone, your dog will turn from an older puppy into a young adult. If you've put in the training and socialization he needed, the tiny eight-week-old puppy you first met will have transformed into a socially accomplished companion who is—mostly—a pleasure to have around. In the course of his training, he should have accepted you as his leader and his guide through any concerns or novelties in his everyday surroundings, and the bond between you should now be solid and will last all his life. And the best aspect of a well-trained dog is that you can take him around quite freely because you know he'll behave well in most situations.

NEW THINGS TO DO

Many smaller dogs will have reached their final height and weight by the end of their first year, and most will get there by the time they are 18 months old. (A handful of the largest breeds may not be physically adult until they hit their second birthday.) Because your pet's bones and muscles are close to being fully grown, you can introduce some different activities that aren't recommended with younger puppies. If you opt to try new things, make sure you build up your pet's exercise regime gradually—you can't expect him to go from small outings and games to two hours of running, say, without having the chance to build up his stamina first.

If you always wanted your dog to be your jogging or cycling buddy, now is the time to try him out. And if he's a natural athlete who has enjoyed every physical activity you've offered him, flyball or agility classes could also be an option.

AGILITY

You may have seen this at local dog shows or on TV. An agility course consists of a range of different equipment arranged in course format. The pieces vary, but there's usually an A-frame, a seesaw, a tunnel, slalom poles, a "pause" table on which your dog's asked to wait for a moment or two at one point on the course, and a number of other pieces. It's a keep-fit challenge for both of you, as you run the course alongside your dog, encouraging him and making sure he takes the obstacles in the right order and tackles them in the right way. Any local dog-training course should be able to direct you to the agility class nearest to you. If you own a small-breed dog don't be put off; this isn't a big-dog-only sport, and most classes can adjust the equipment to suit smaller dogs if necessary.

Grown - up Play

Along with humans, dogs are one of just a handful of species who play for pleasure after they mature. In many species, play is purely functional: a rehearsal for the lessons a young animal needs to learn to survive. Like us, however, dogs appear to play purely to entertain themselves and as a way of engaging with other members—whether human or canine—of their "pack."

FLYBALL

This is a great sport for smart, sociable dogs who love to be part of a team. It requires the dogs to race along a line of hurdles, put their paw on a small platform which causes a tennis ball to be released, catch the ball, then race back along the hurdles with the ball in their mouth and deliver it to their owner on the finish line. Although your dog may practice on his own, flyball clubs feature regular team practice and competitions that pit teams of dogs (usually four on each team) against one another. Again, small dogs can compete as well as large ones; the height of the hurdles is decided by the shoulder height of the smallest dog competing, and mixed teams are common.

If you think your dog would enjoy either activity, ask a local club if you can do a few rounds as a tryout. Some classes require your pet to hold a certificate from a basic obedience class before you can join. It will take him a little time to grasp the idea behind the courses, but most dogs enjoy figuring it out, and you may find that you've discovered an activity you can share all his active life.

7"

SETTLING DOWN

Now that your dog is maturing, you're likely to find that he's more able to settle for an hour or two while you're working or your attention is simply elsewhere. Even though he's no longer demanding your attention, you should still remember to fix him up with activities that will keep him happy and occupied during downtime. Boredom is as bad for dogs as it is for people, and there are a number of things that can keep him occupied that don't require your supervision. Raw, meaty bones are great for his teeth; on a sunny day, a marrowbone will keep him happily absorbed for several hours. And heavy, hollow rubber toys such as Kongs, stuffed with food that your pet has to gradually get out, are equally popular with many dogs. In hot weather, you can even turn these into canine ice pops by pouring gravy into them and putting them in the freezer for a few hours: your dog will enjoy the resulting cool treat. Trick toys with treats inside that he can only get at by manipulating them and working out how to get the treats out are another good way to keep him busy—some dogs master them right away, while others take a long time to work them out.

TRAINING FOR LIFE

Even though, at over a year old, some dogs may well be considered "trained," in that they understand the various things asked of them and generally are obedient when you need them to be—it will take others a little longer—never abandon training exercises altogether. Even if you no longer need to run through your pet's "sit" and "stay" sequences every day, be sure to give him a short training session every so often to keep him topped up and ensure that he remembers that he needs to listen to you. Some dogs genuinely love training and the engagement with you that it offers; if yours is one of them, consider teaching him more complex tricks and games—not only will he enjoy learning them, but an extensive repertoire of tricks will make him a popular performer—and most dogs love the applause and laughter that greets a good trick. In fact, many dogs will try running through the various things they know, in sequence and unasked, if they think someone near them may have a reward to offer.

GLOSSARY

Aggression: Forceful, threatening behavior meant to repel or intimidate.

Agility: A sports activity in which a dog negotiates an obstacle course with his owner running alongside him. Agility contests are run against the clock. Not recommended for dogs under a year old.

BARF diet: The Bones and Raw Food diet for dogs; a variant of raw feeding. Enthusiasts believe that it is the most natural option for dogs, and the one that is best for their health. Some versions include vegetables; others consist purely of meat and bones.

Breed: A classification based on a dog's heritage and parentage. Most breeds have formal classifications registered with some or all of the national kennel clubs.

Coat: A dog's outer hair covering. Coats may be "double," with a hard top layer and a soft undercoat, or "single," the top layer only. A dog's coat type is dictated by its breed and parentage.

Colostrum: The milk that a mother dog or dam feeds her litter for the day directly after its birth. As well as being rich in nutrients, it contains antibodies that give the puppies a degree of immunity against infection.

Counter-conditioning: A way of desensitizing a puppy to things that worry him by creating a positive association with them—for example, feeding him treats while running a noisy vacuum cleaner might act as counter-conditioning against the puppy's fear of the vacuum.

Crate/puppy crate: A portable cage made of plastic and metal, used to contain or transport a dog. Available in various sizes; dividers can be used to make a crate smaller while a puppy is growing, and then removed when the dog is full-grown.

Crepuscular: The habit of being most active at the beginning and the end of the day. Historically, dogs are crepuscular and even domesticated dogs may remain most active early in the morning and in the evening.

Dog daycare: Daily boarding for pets whose owners work. Dogs are dropped off in the morning and collected in the evening, mix together in groups, and are taken for walks in the course of the day.

Extender leash: A leash that extends to a length of several yards when a button is held and retracts when it is released. Intended to give a dog some degree of freedom on walks where recall may be an issue. Not suitable for use as a training leash.

Fear period/Fear impact period: An established period or periods in a puppy's development when he becomes fearful of the unknown and very cautious about any unfamiliar object or experience. There are usually two distinct fear impact periods during puppyhood, the first when the puppy is aged between eight and 12 weeks, and the second as he approaches adolescence at around six months.

Flyball: A sports activity in which dogs run a course over hurdles, collect a ball and return over the hurdles to bring it to their owner or handler. Not recommended for dogs under a year old.

Hot spot: An area of inflamed and irritated skin on a puppy that usually results from an allergy to flea saliva. If a puppy is suffering from a hot spot or spots he should be taken to the vet for treatment urgently.

Housetraining/housebreaking: The process by which a puppy is trained to toilet outside.

Immunity: The capability of the body to resist disease. Young puppies gain a degree of immunity through the colostrum fed to them by their mothers; their immunity must subsequently be strengthened by a series of injections given by a veterinarian.

Imprinting window/imprinting period: The first 16 weeks of a puppy's life, during which he is learning at a huge rate, and in the course of which experiences make the greatest impact on his development.

Long line/training line: A long cord with a collar clip on one end, used in training. Intended to give the puppy freedom to move around while practicing recall or socializing with other dogs, but to allow his handler to pick up the end if it is necessary to restrain him for any reason.

Microchip: A device the size of a grain of rice, inserted by a vet under a puppy's skin between the shoulder blades. It contains a unique number that can be read by a scanner, and enables lost pets to be identified and returned to their owners. In some countries microchipping of all dogs is compulsory.

Mixed breed: A dog whose parents are either of different purebreds or are mixed-breed.

Neutering: Sterilizing a male dog by removing its testicles.

Pack leader: Term originally used by scientists to identify the alpha member of a pack of animals, in particular wolves. Used both of a dog who behaves and acts as "leader" of their pack, or the person who a dog views as his pack leader.

Pin brush: A grooming brush with wire teeth topped with soft rubber tips so the puppy's hair is not pulled too much during brushing.

Puppy mill: A set-up for the intensive breeding of puppies, run purely for profit, usually in inhumane and overcrowded conditions. The puppies produced in a puppy mill are usually sold to pet shops, dealers, and sometimes online.

Puppy party: A meet-and-greet session for young dogs, giving them the opportunity to socialize as a group. Usually organized by a vet's surgery or a puppy training class

Puppy pen/exercise pen: Similar to a child's playpen, with closely spaced bars so the puppy is safely contained.

Purebred: A dog with two parents of the same breed.

Rescue: An organization that rescues unwanted dogs, either handed in by their owners or found stray, and rehomes them. May accept any breed of dog or be breed-specific.

Resource guarding: When a dog behaves possessively and potentially aggressively around a valued resource, such as food or a toy. Careful training in puppyhood can usually eliminate this, although some dogs have a much stronger tendency to resource-guard than others.

Shedding: The process by which a dog loses excess hair from its coat. Heavy shedding is often seasonal, but some breeds shed continuously, year round, while others shed relatively little.

Shelter: The kennels where rescue organizations keep their dogs while advertising them for rehoming.

Socialization: The exposure of a puppy to new experiences of every kind, from other dogs to unknown people and places, to aid in his positive development.

Spaying: Sterilizing a female dog by removing its ovaries and uterus.

Submissive urination: When a young dog urinates as a sign of submission to a senior dog or a human.

Temperament: The key personality traits of a puppy. Temperament testing is often done by breeders before puppies are released to their new homes, and is almost always carried out when a puppy is being put up for adoption by a rescue organization.

Vaccination: A series of injections given to stimulate a puppy's immune system, to protect it against infection.

Verbal cue: The word or phrase associated with a trained behavior, such as "sit" or "stay."

FURTHER READING

Aloff, Brenda. *Canine Body Language: A Photographic Guide*. Wenatchee, WA: Dogwise Publishing, 2009.

Aloff, Brenda. *Puppy Problems? No Problem!* Wenatchee, WA: Dogwise Publishing, 2012.

Anderson, Teoti. *Your Outta Control Puppy*. Neptune City, NJ: T.F.H. Publications, 2003.

Bradshaw, John. *In Defence of Dogs*. New York, NY: Penguin, 2012.

Clothier, Suzanne. *Bones Would Rain From the Sky: Deepening Our Relationships with Dogs*. New York, NY: Warner Books, 2002.

Coren, Stanley. *How to Speak Dog*. New York, NY: Simon & Schuster, 2001.

Dunbar, Ian. *Before and After Getting Your Puppy*. Novato, CA: New World Library, 2004.

Fennell, Jan. *The Dog Listener*. New York, NY: HarperCollins, 2004.

Fisher, John. *Think Dog: An Owner's Guide to Canine Psychology*. London: Cassell Illustrated, 2012.

Hetts, Suzanne & Estep, Daniel. *Raising a Behaviorally Healthy Puppy: A Pet Parenting Guide*. Littleton CO: Island Dog Press, 2005.

Horowitz, Debra F., Ciribassi, John and Dale, Steve. *Decoding Your Dog*. Boston, MA: Houghton Mifflin Harcourt, 2014.

London, Karen B. & McConnell, Patricia B. *Play Together, Stay Together: Happy and Healthy Play Between People and Dogs*. Black Earth, WI: McConnell Publishing, 2008.

Lorenz, Konrad. *Man Meets Dog*. Boston, MA: Houghton Mifflin Co., 1955.

McConnell, Patricia B. *How to Be the Leader of the Pack and Have Your Dog Love You For It*. Black Earth, WI: McConnell Publishing, 2007.

McConnell, Patricia B. *The Other End of the Leash: Why We Do What We Do Around Dogs*. New York, NY: Ballantine, 2002.

McConnell, Patricia B. & Skidmore, Brenda. *The Puppy Primer*. Black Earth, WI: McConnell Publishing, 2010.

Miller, Pat. *Love Your Dog, Train Your Dog*. Wenatchee, WA: Dogwise Publishing, 2004.

Miller, Pat. *Play With Your Dog*. Wenatchee, WA: Dogwise Publishing, 2008.

Rugaas, Turid. *On Talking Terms with Dogs, Calming Signals*. Wenatchee, WA: Dogwise Publishing, 2006.

Stilwell, Victoria. *Train Your Dog Positively*. Berkeley, CA: Ten Speed Press, 2014.

Sullivan, Karen. *Get Fit with Your Dog*. Hauppauge, NY: Barron's Educational Series, 2008.

Yin, Sophia. *How to Behave So Your Dog Behaves*. Neptune City, NJ: T.F.H. Publications, 2004.

PICTURE CREDITS

INDEX